THE ART OF MANDALA

COLORING BOOK

TH BOOK BELONG TO :

COLOR TEST PAGE

ARE YOU READY ?

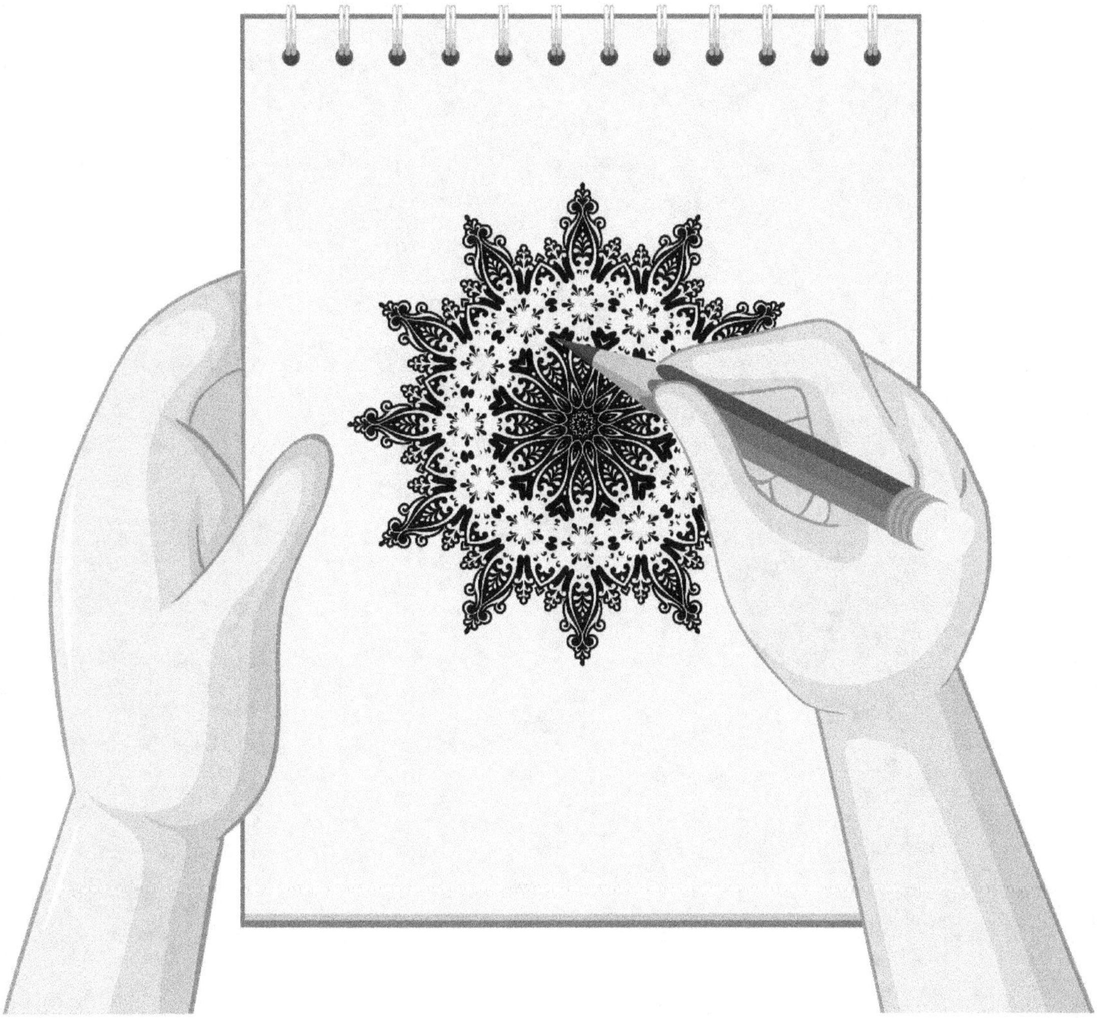

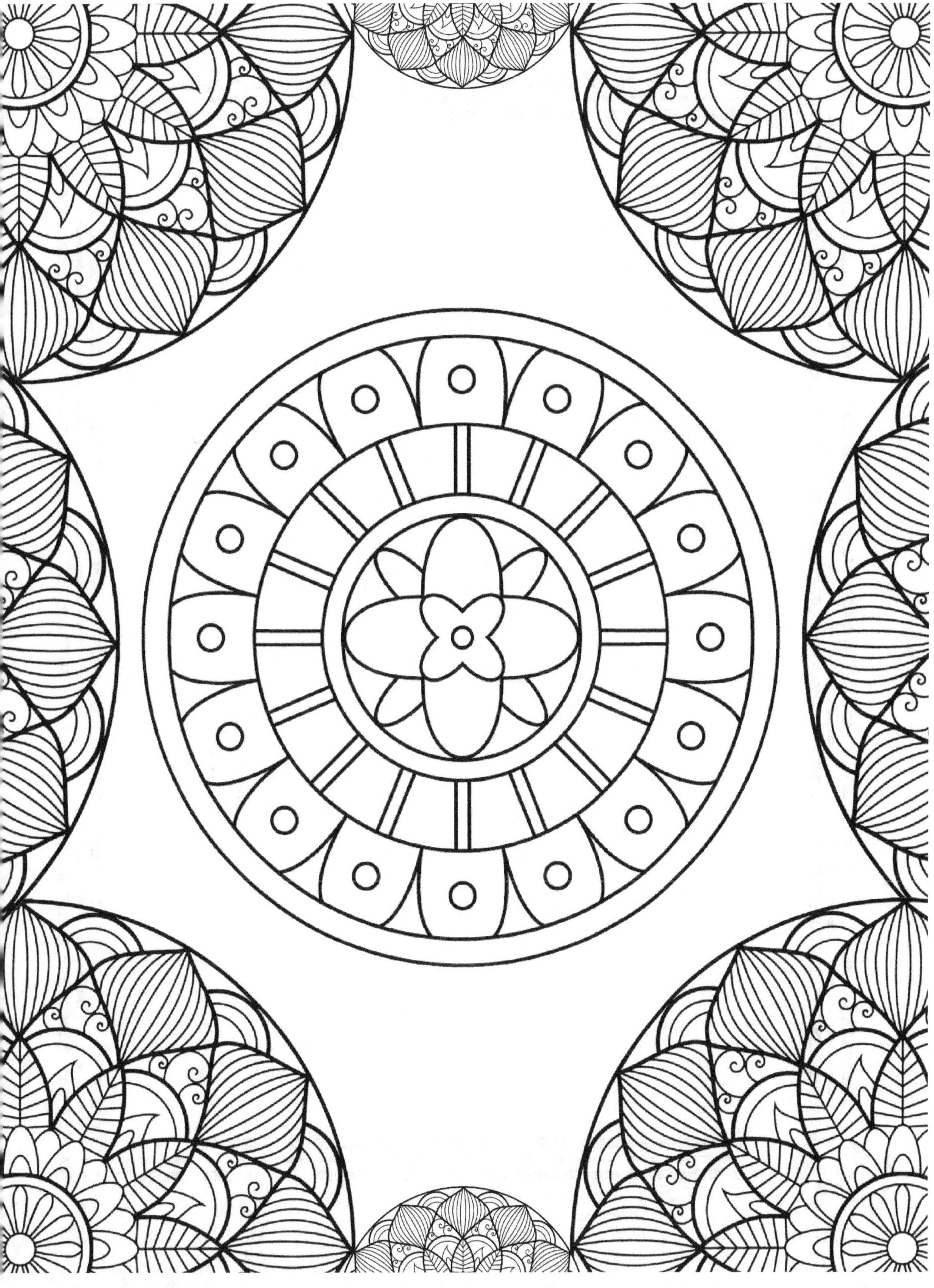

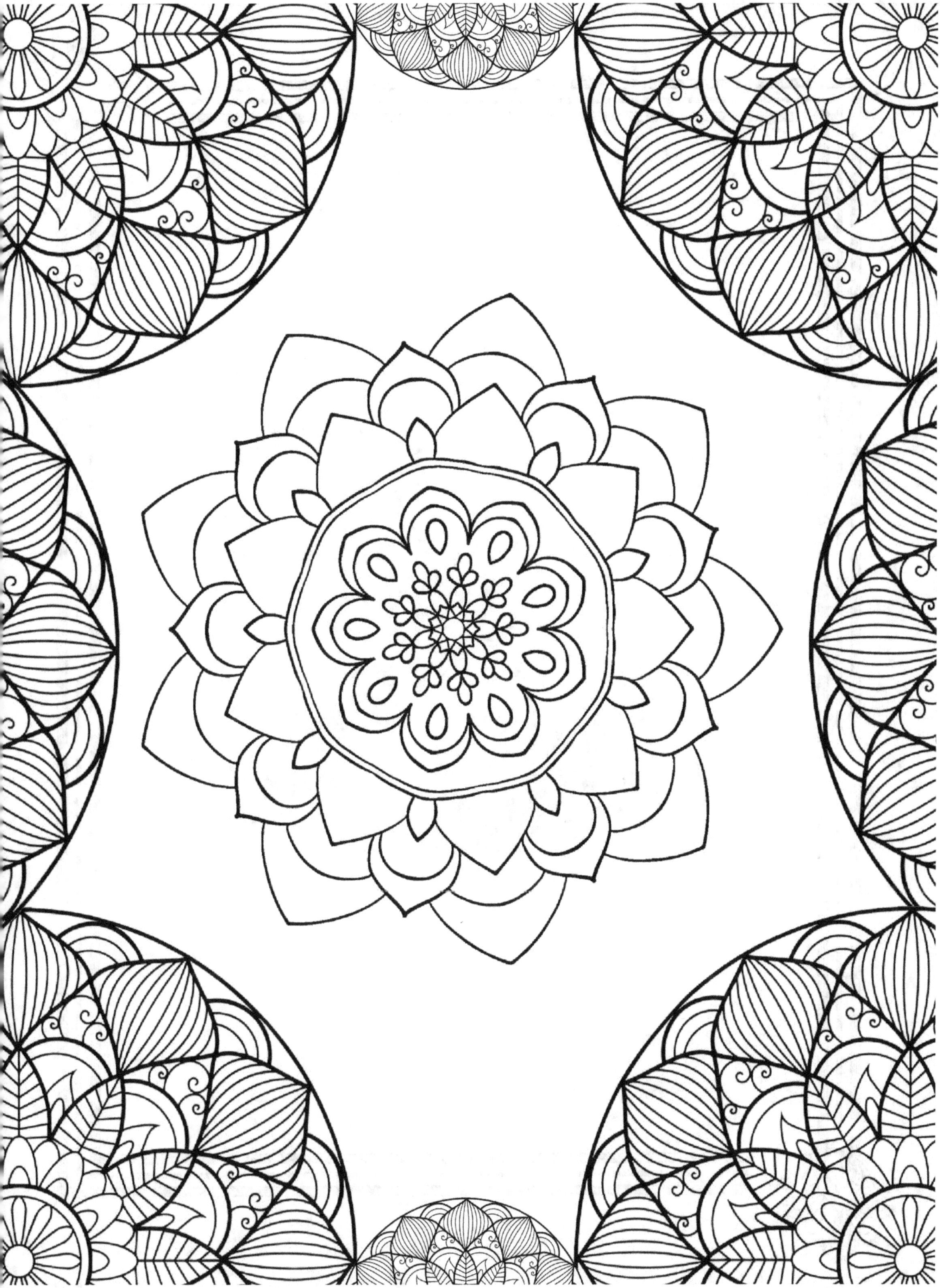

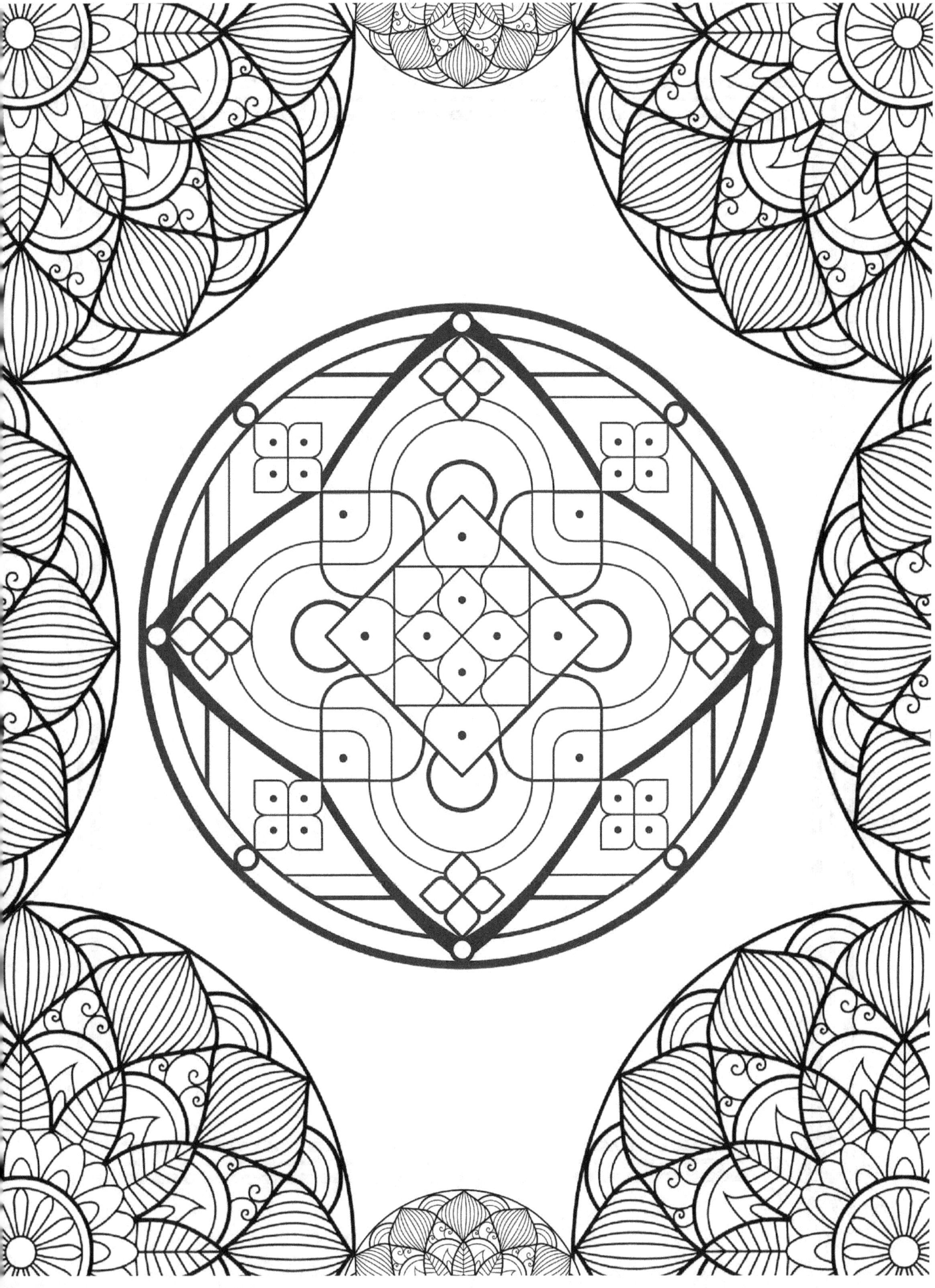

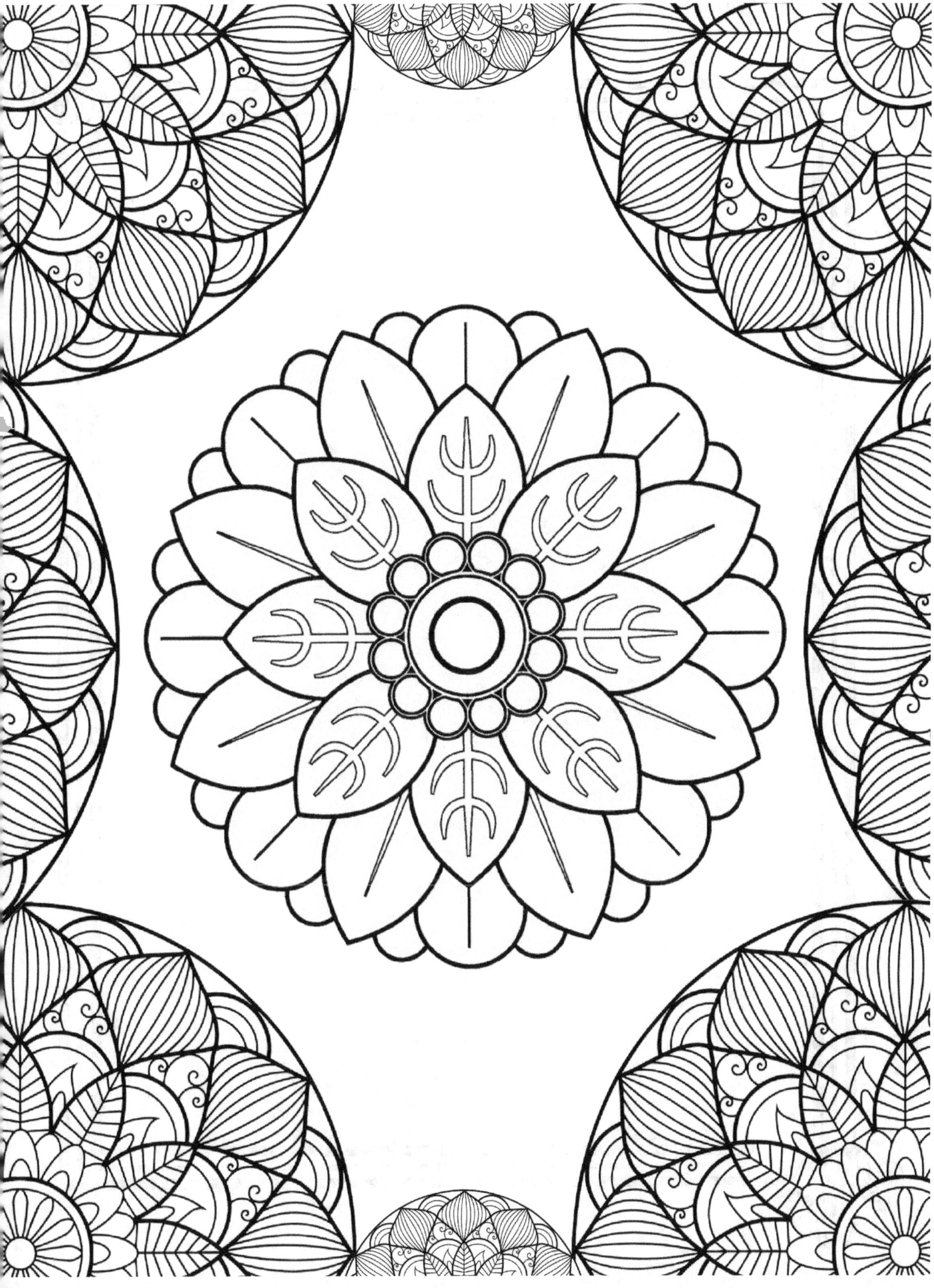

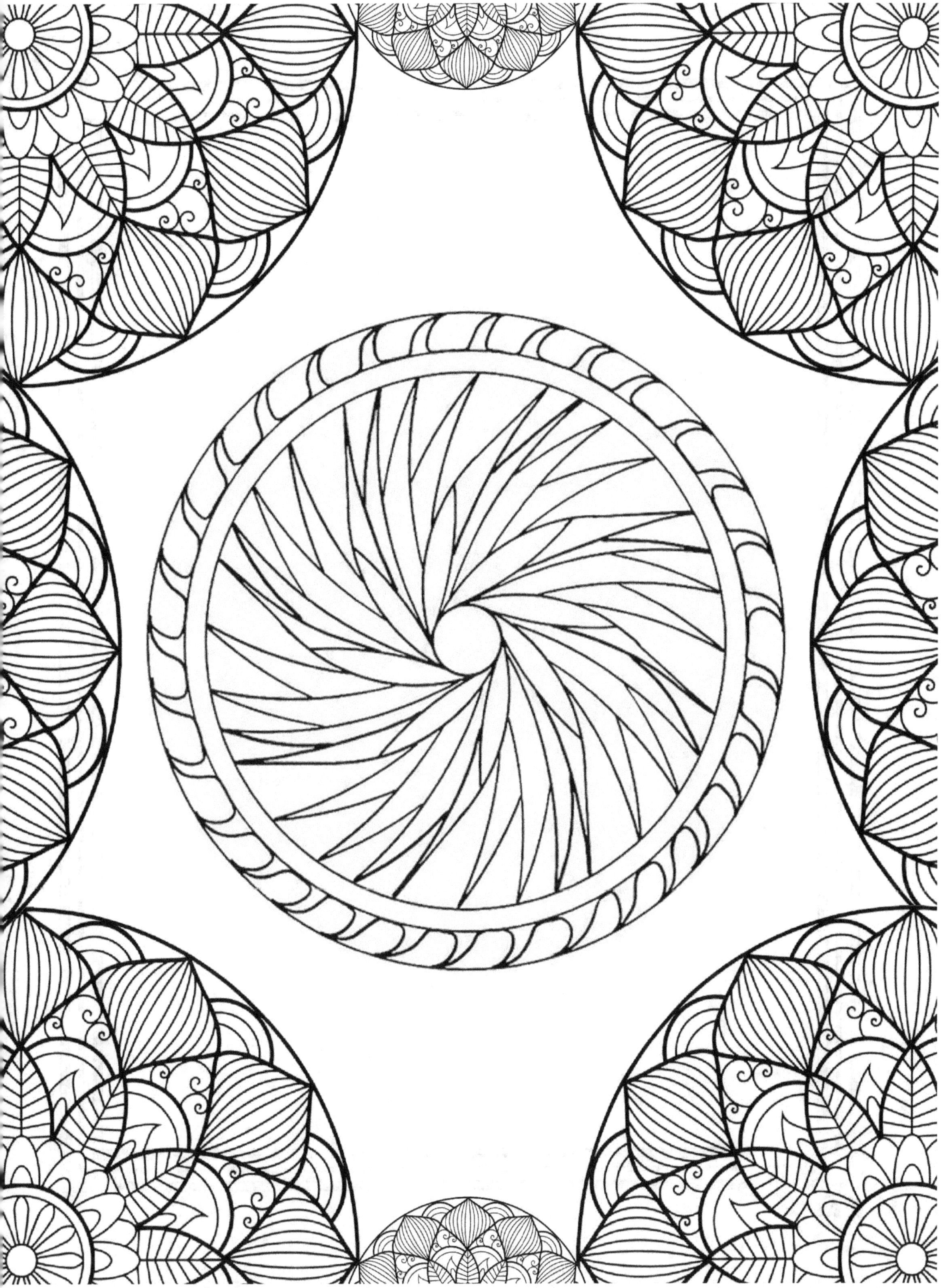

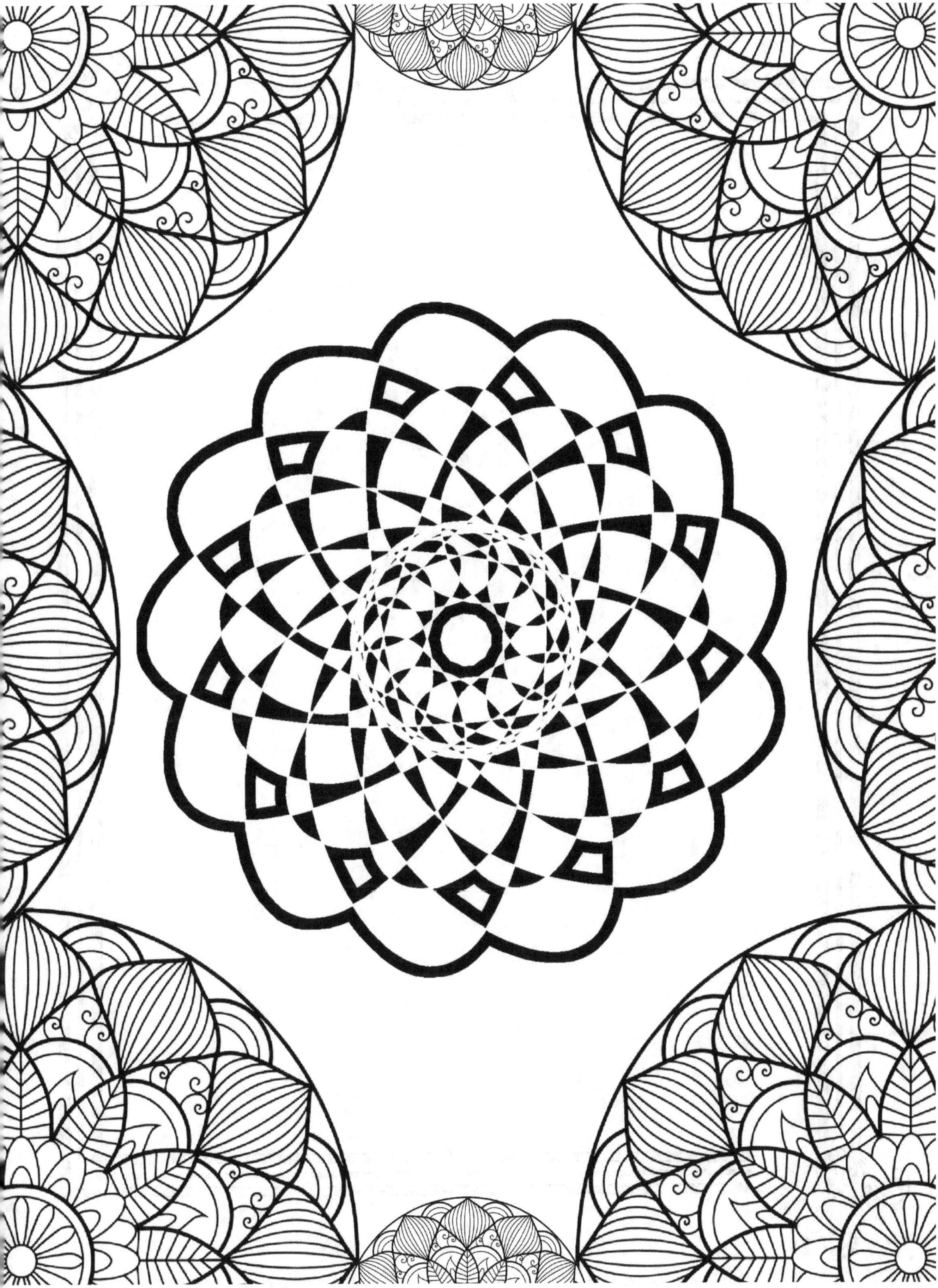

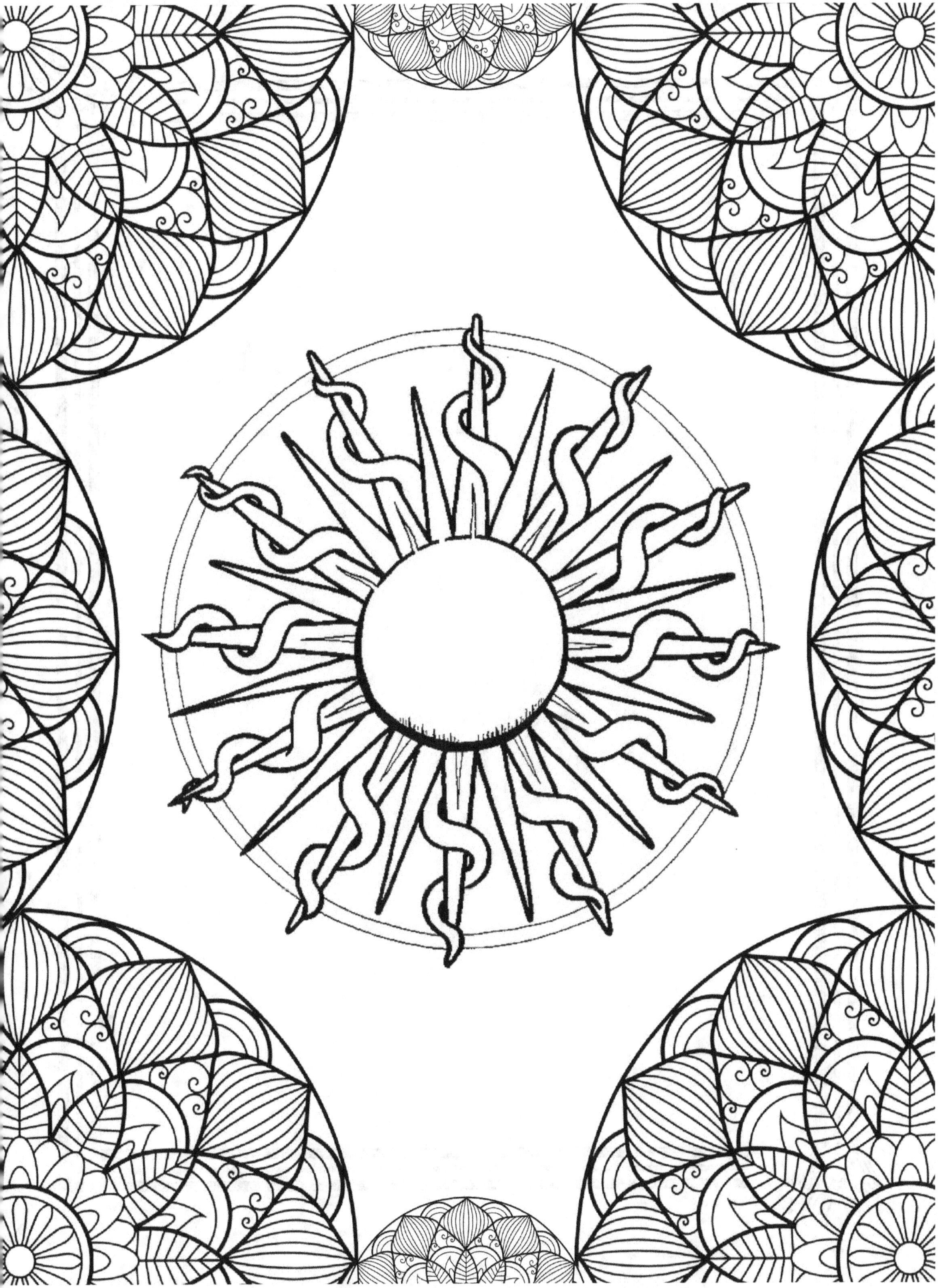

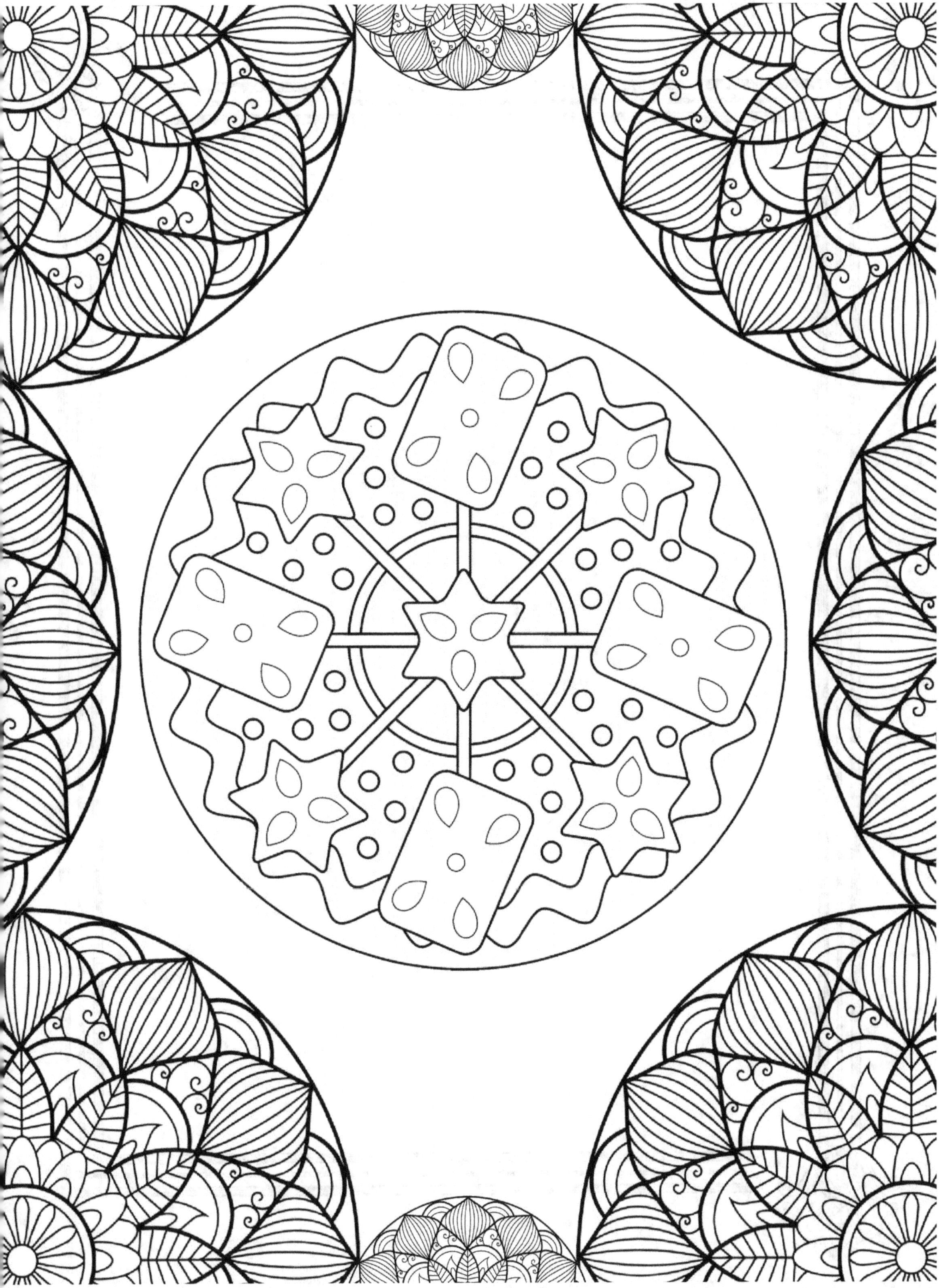

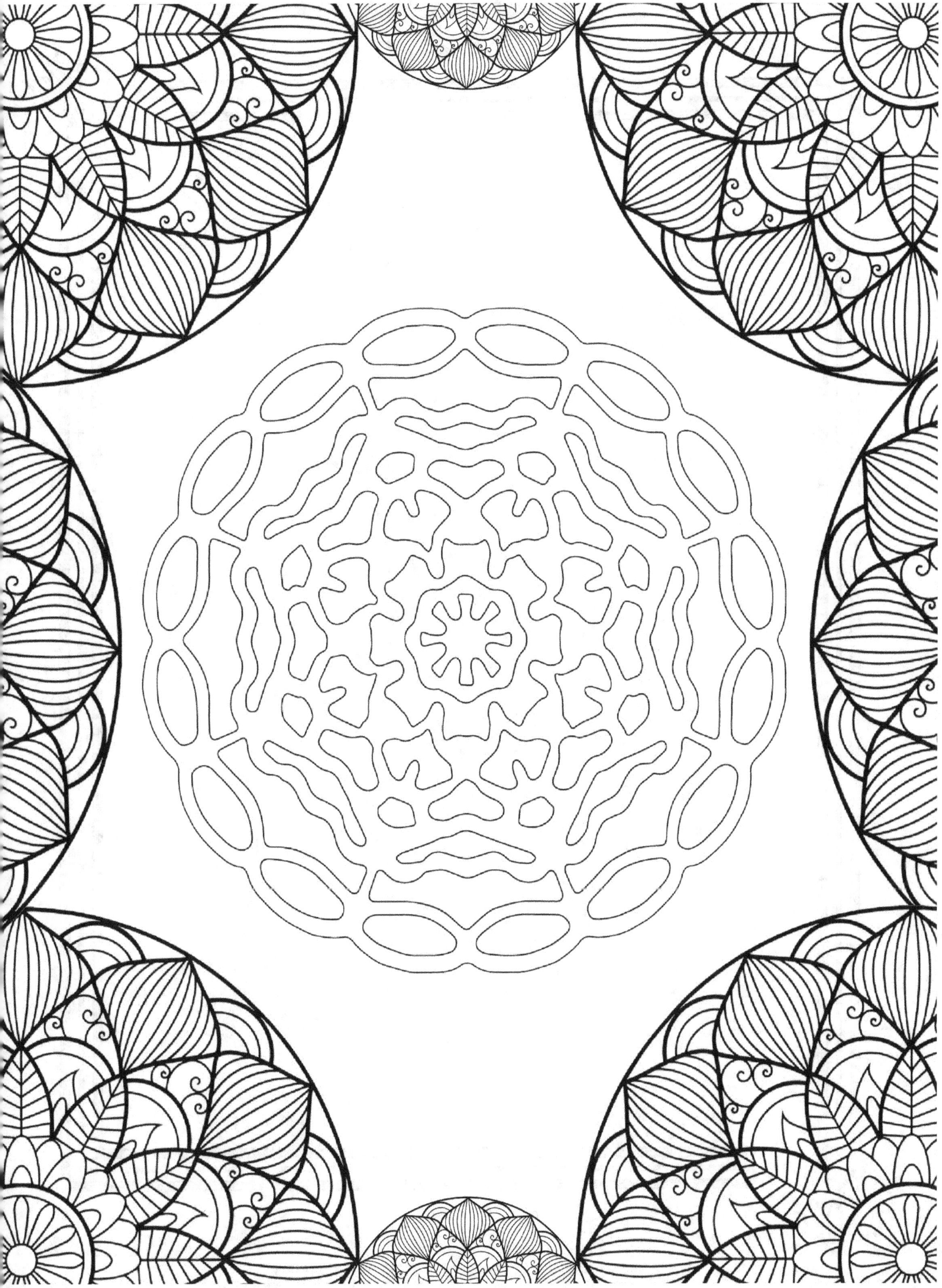

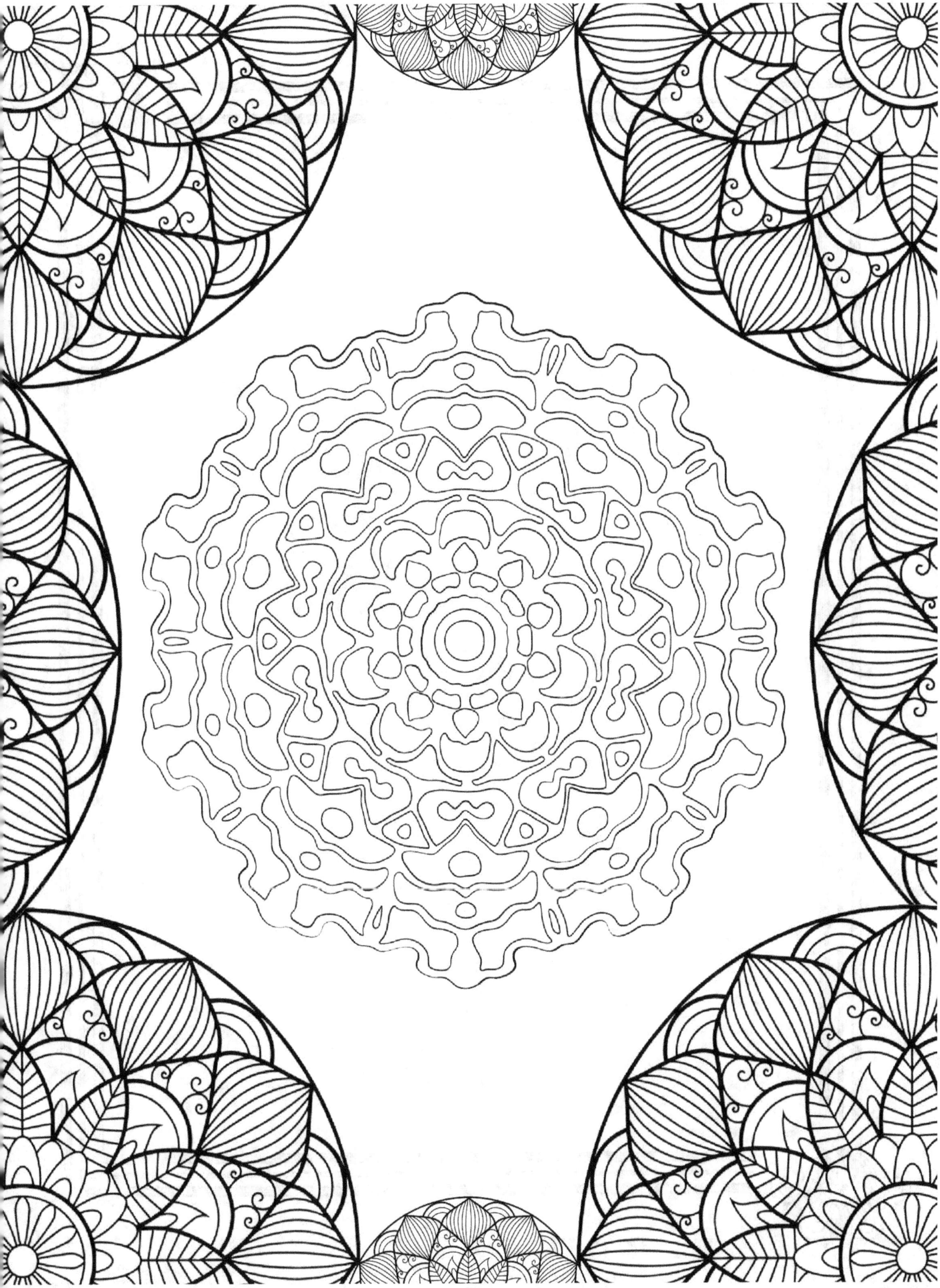

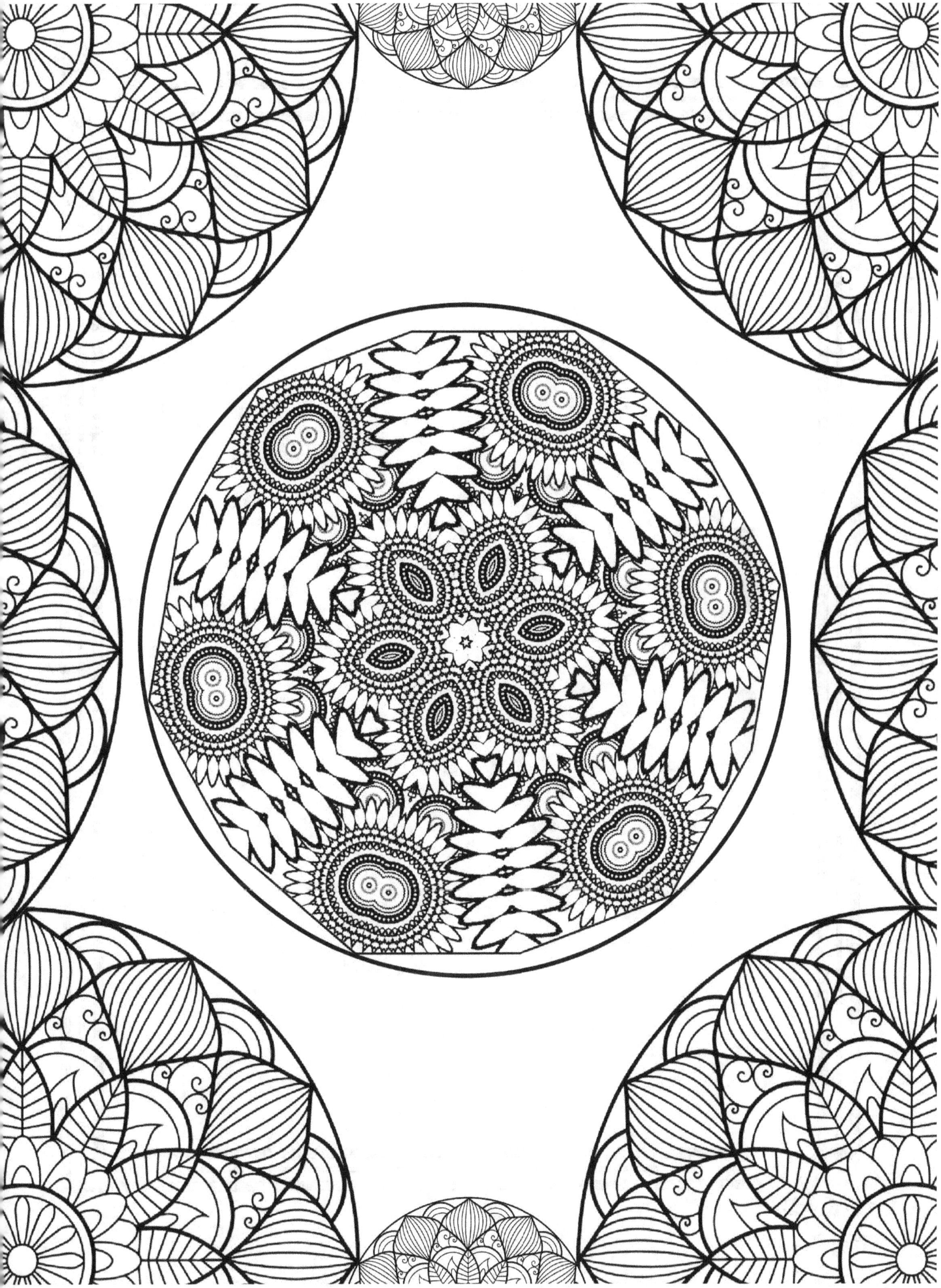

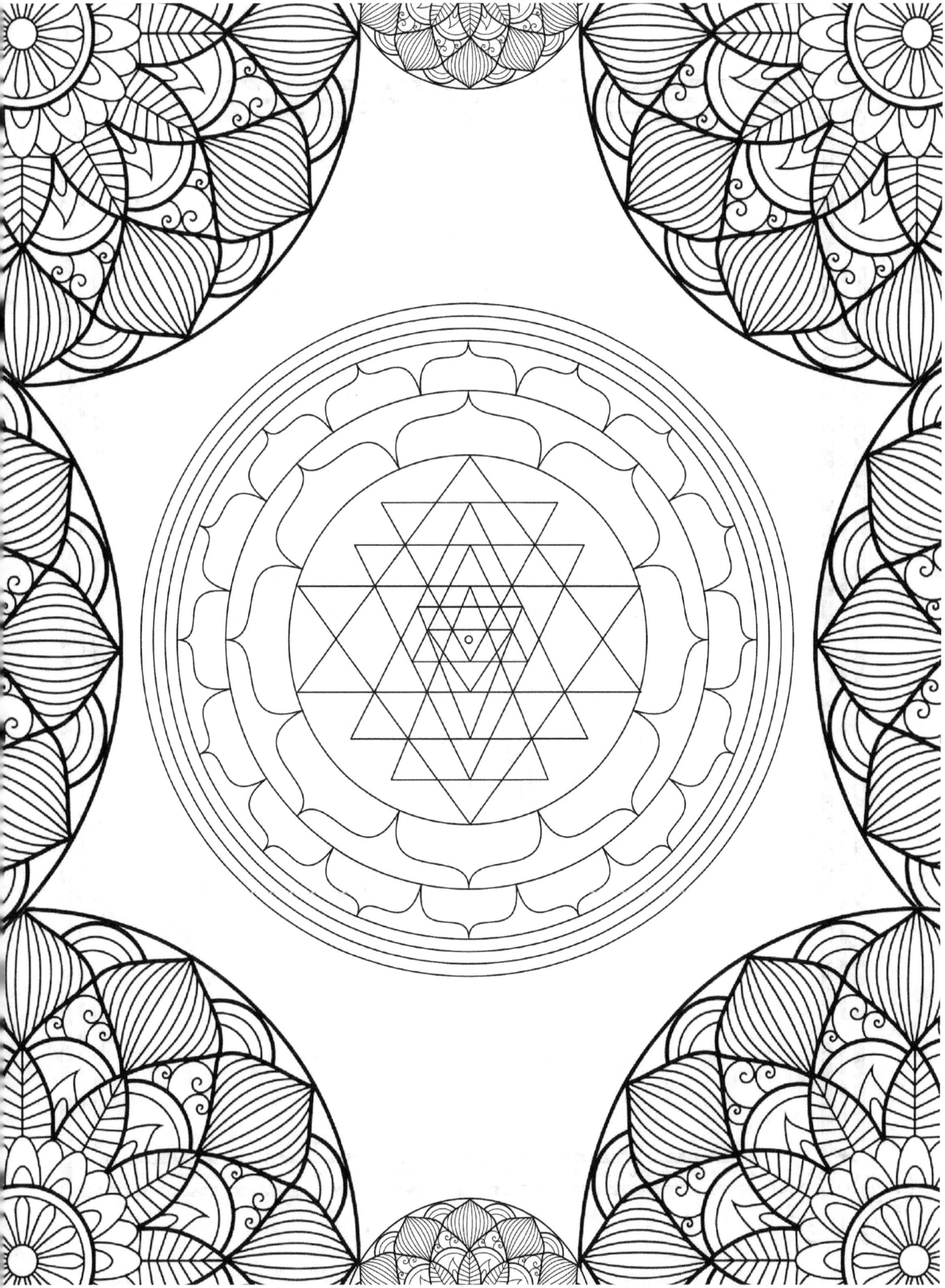

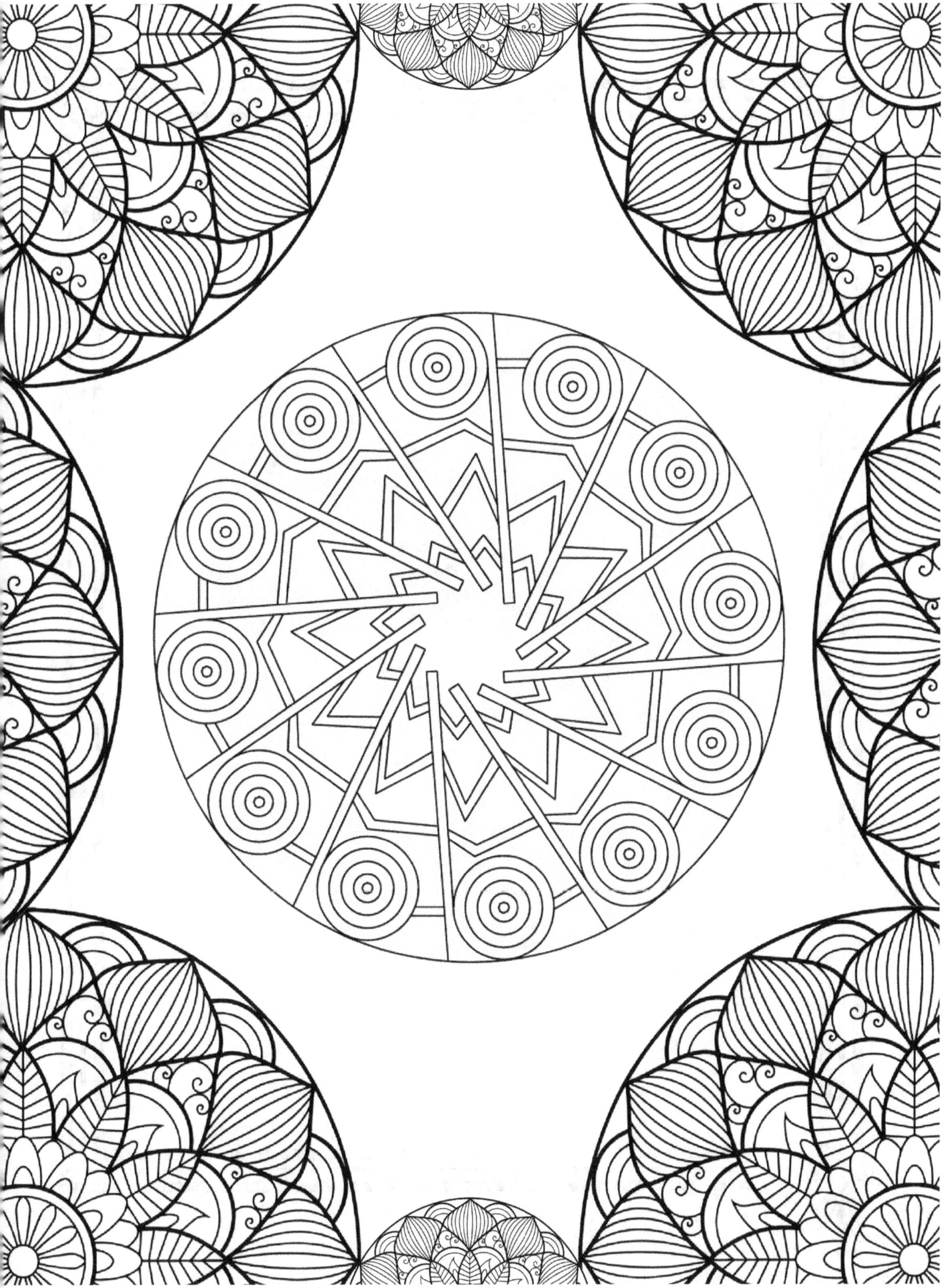

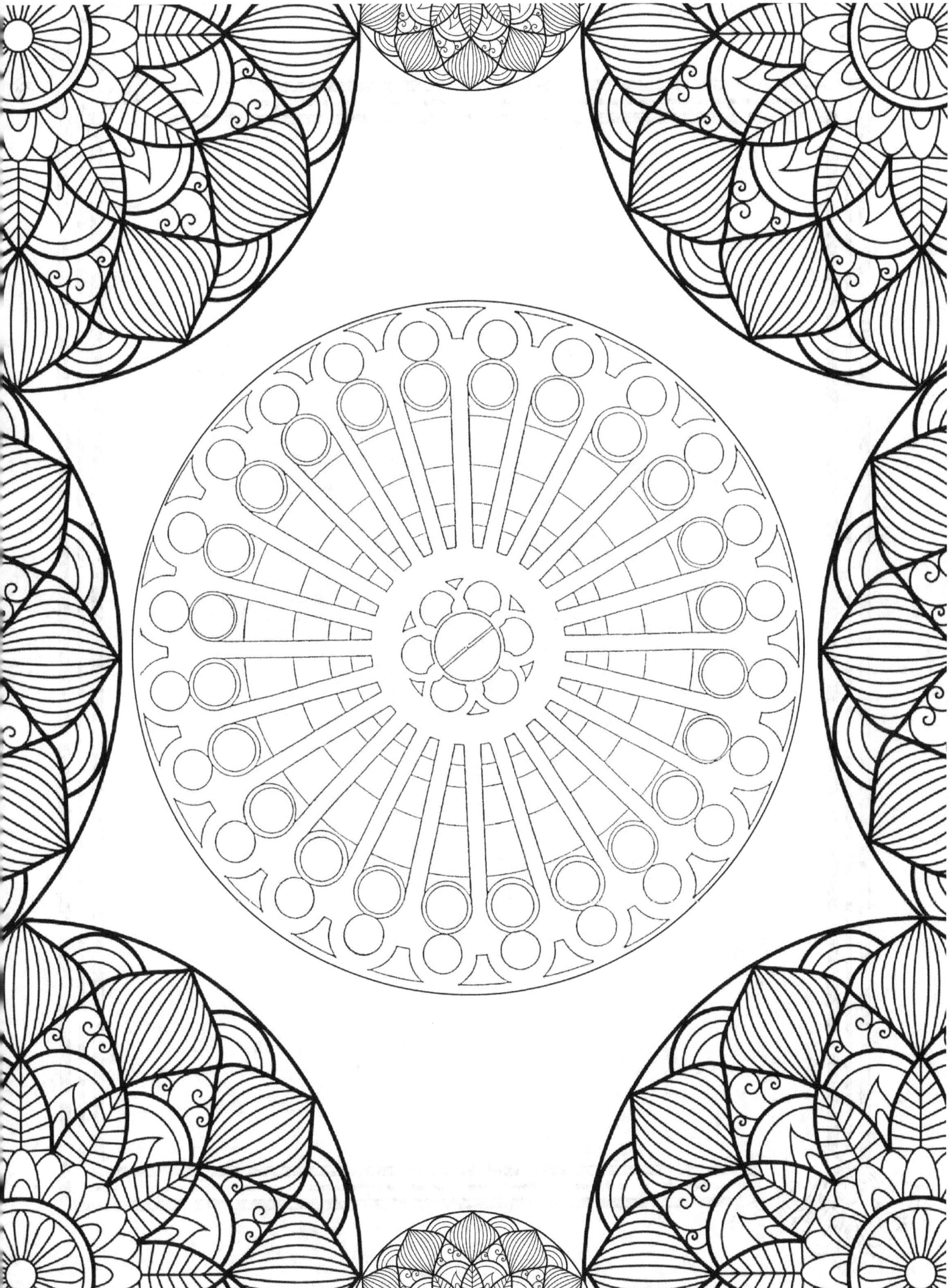

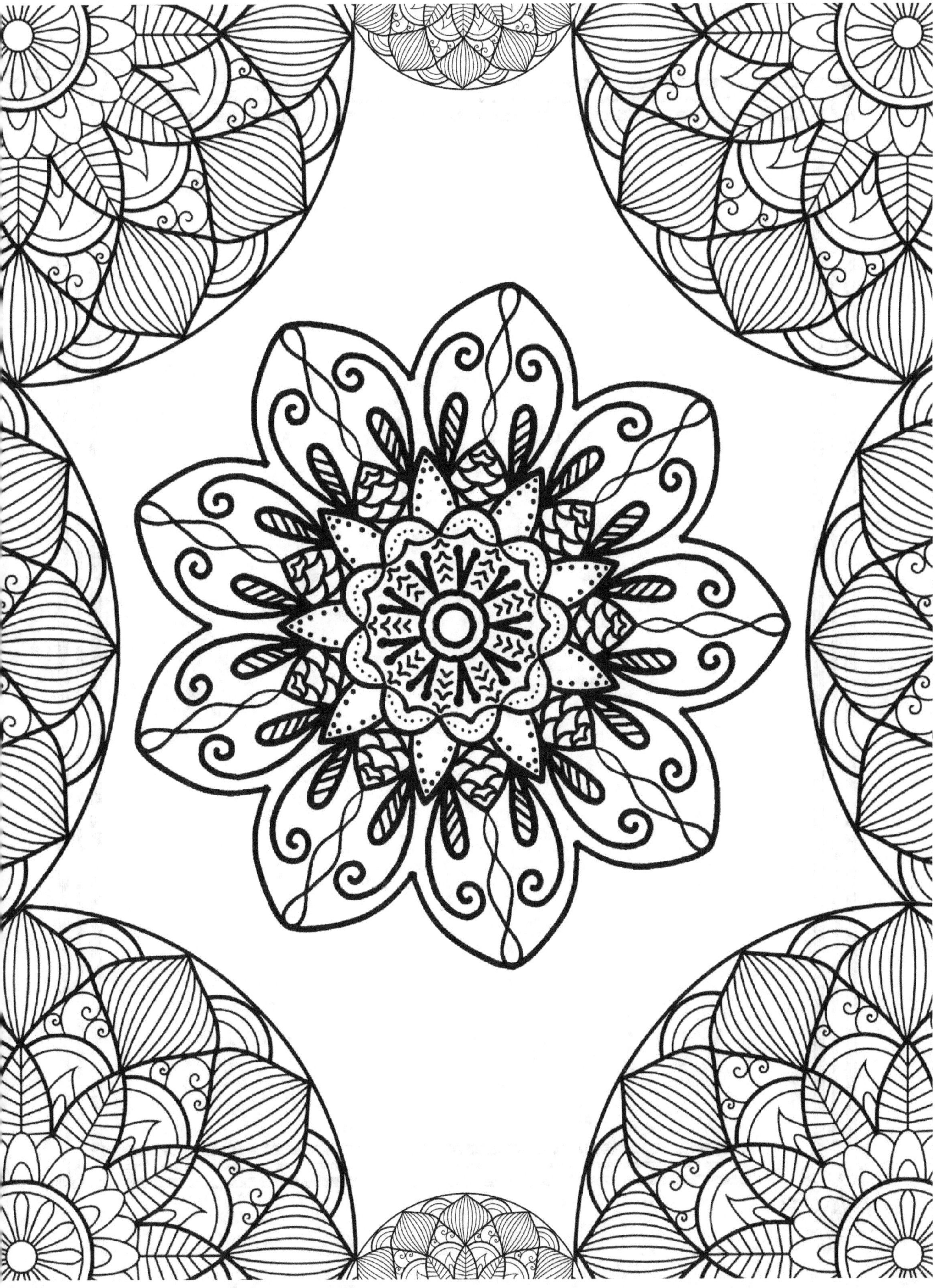

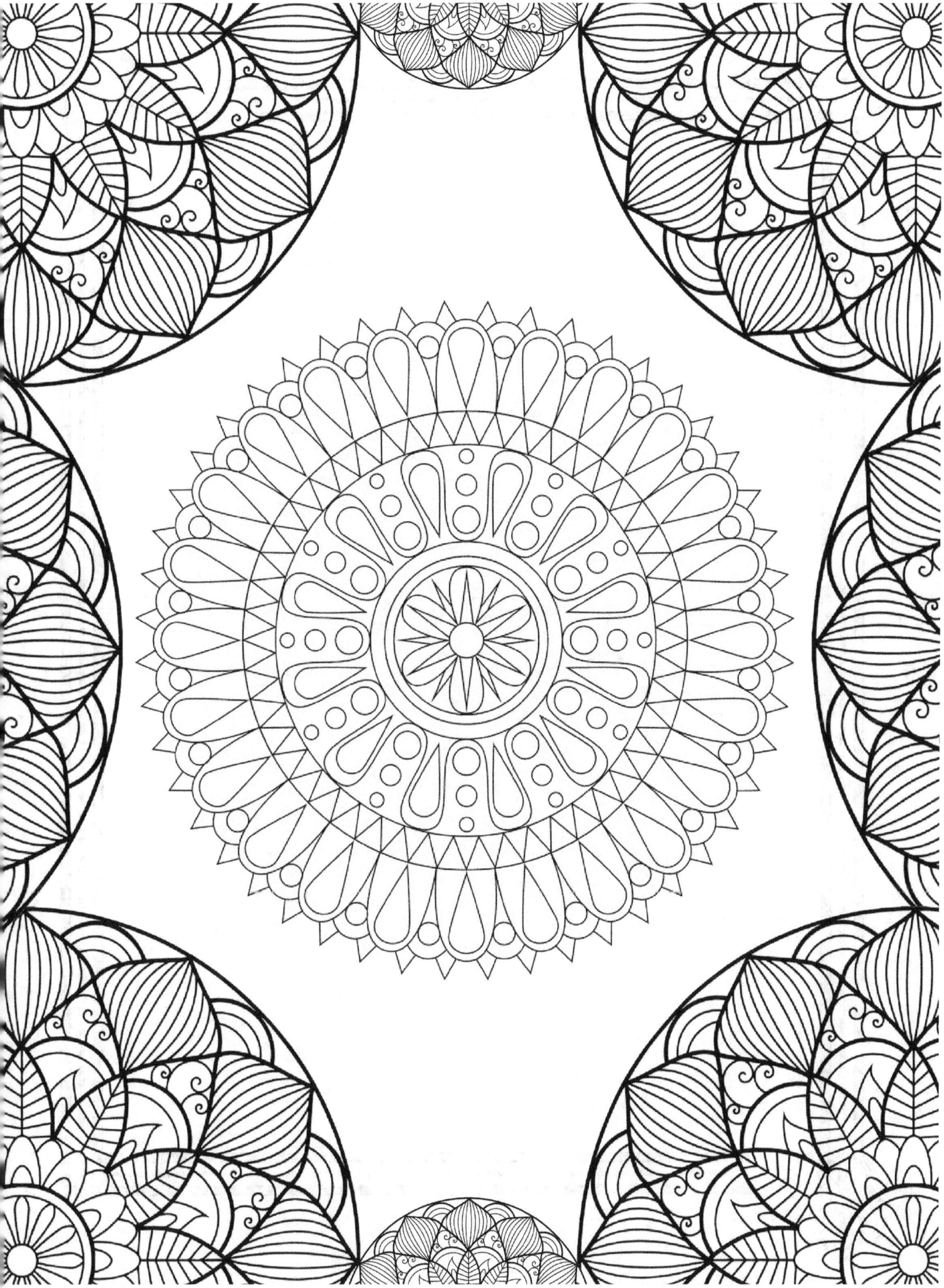

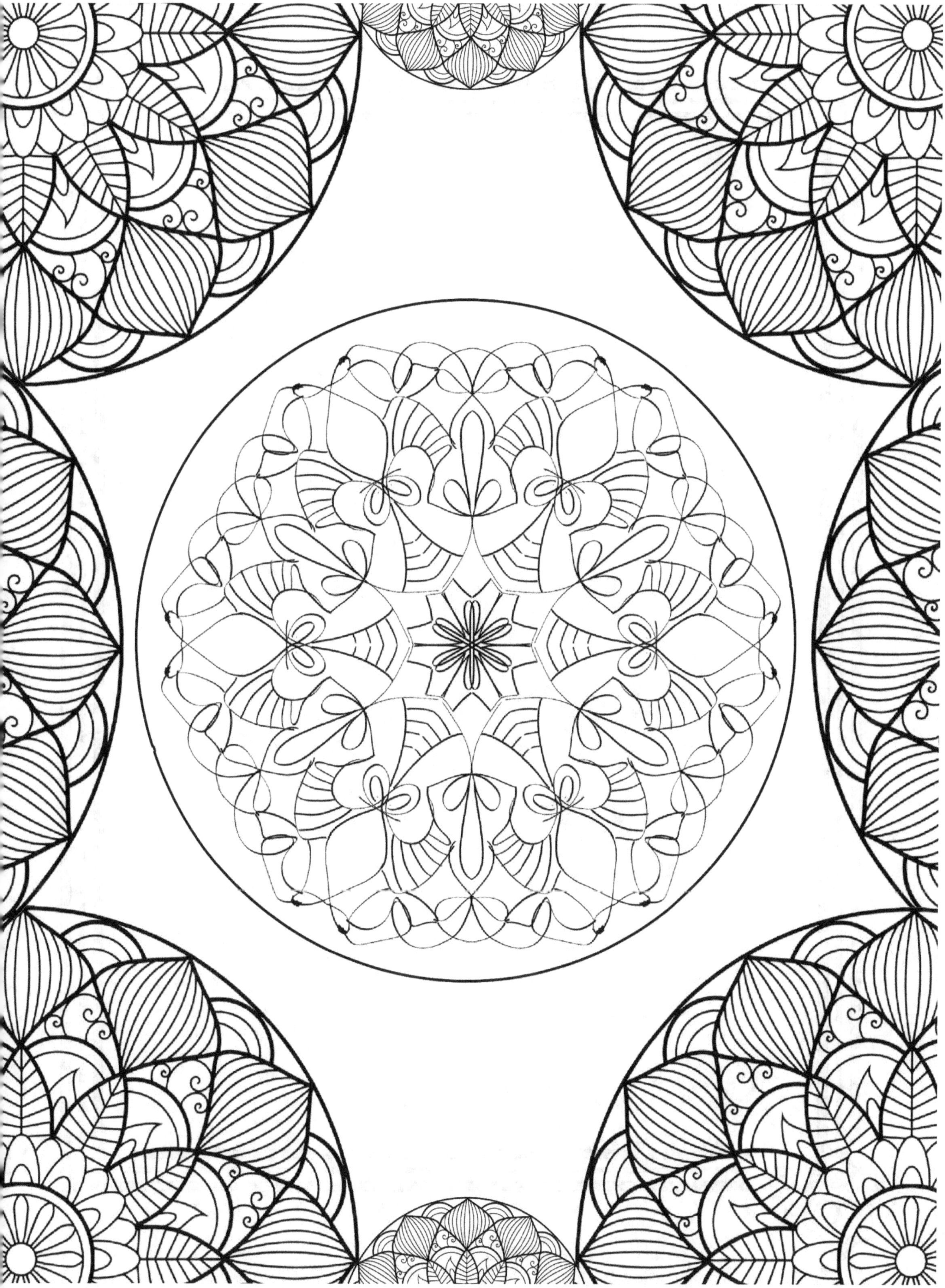

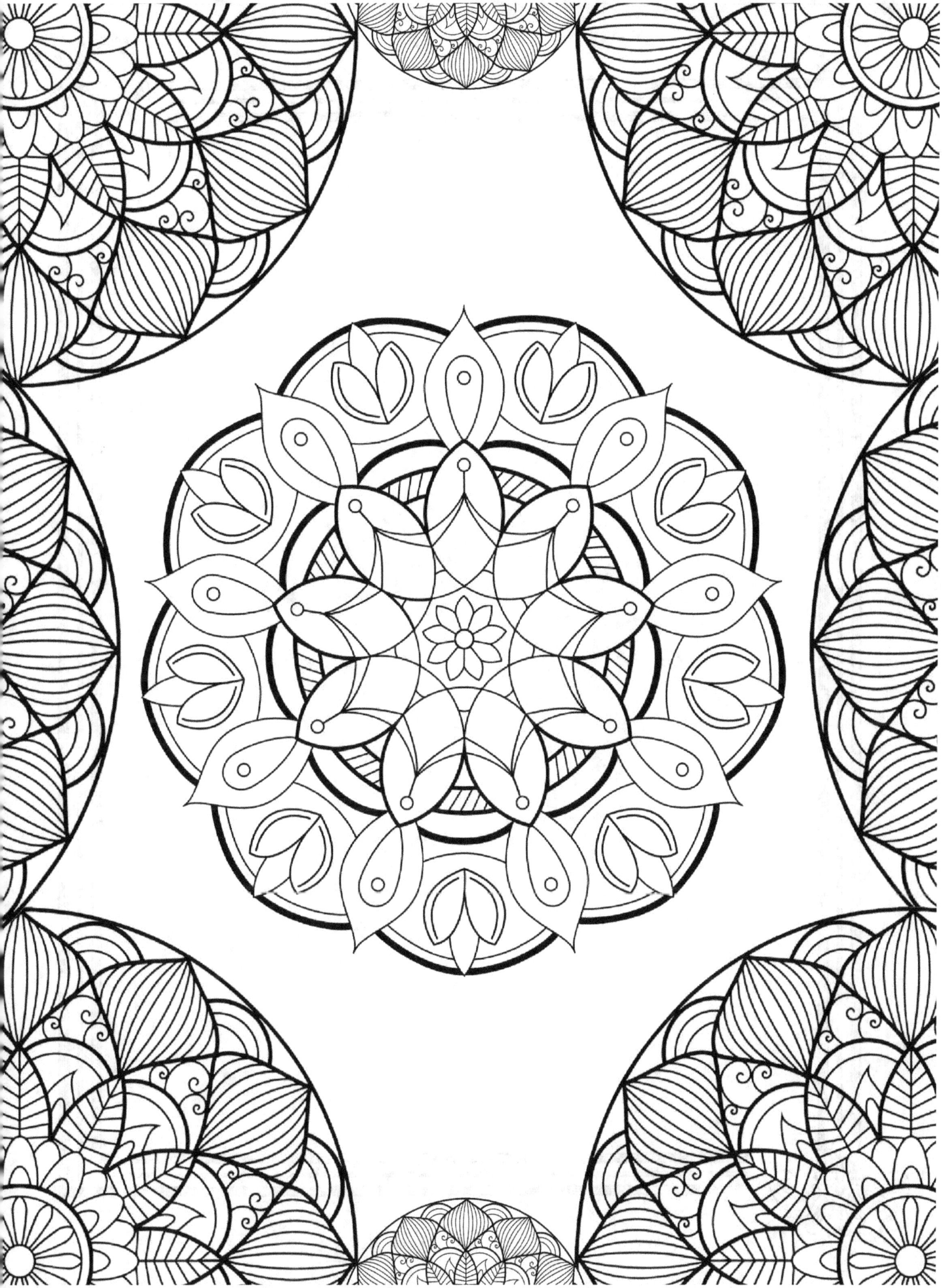

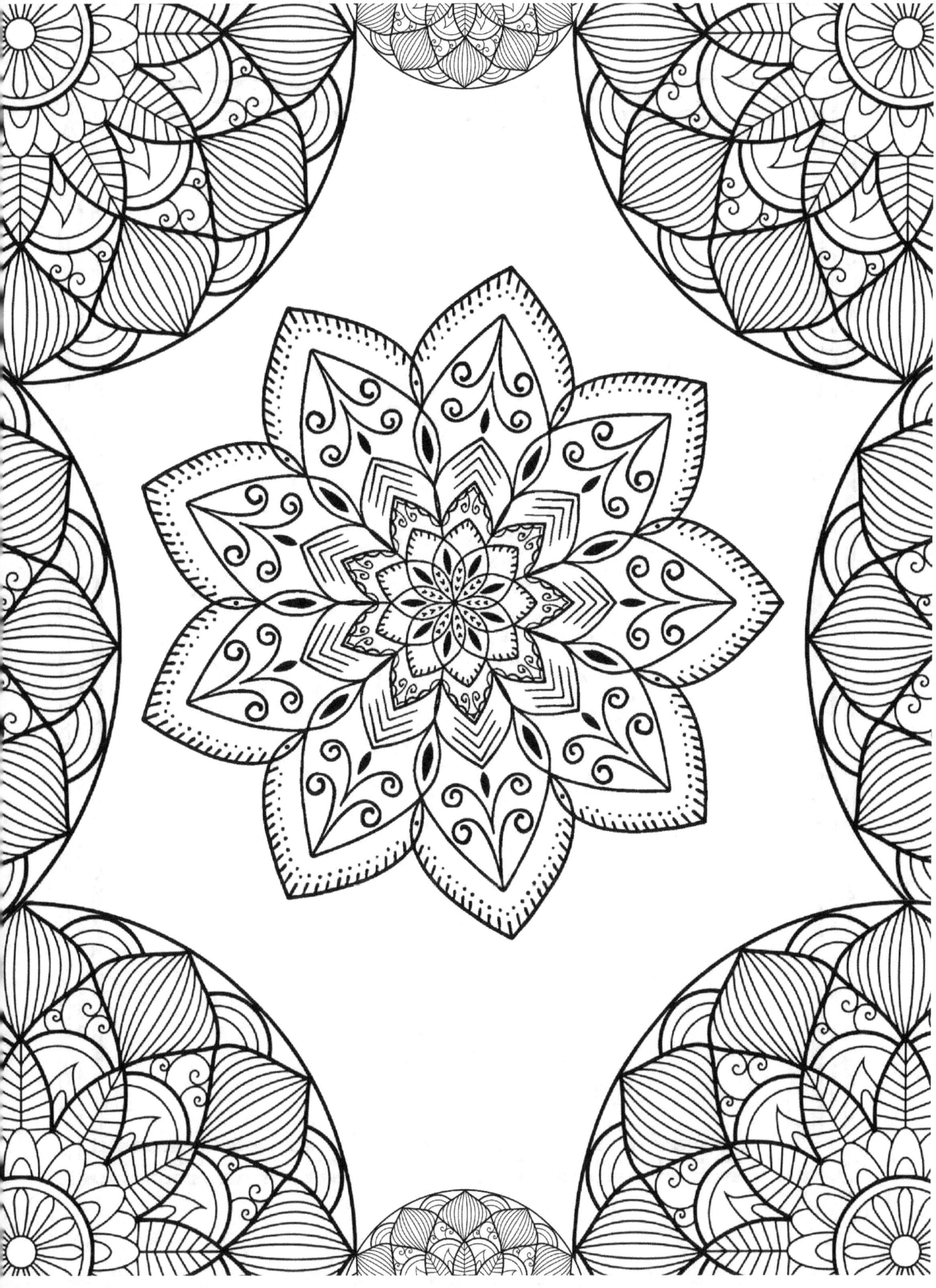

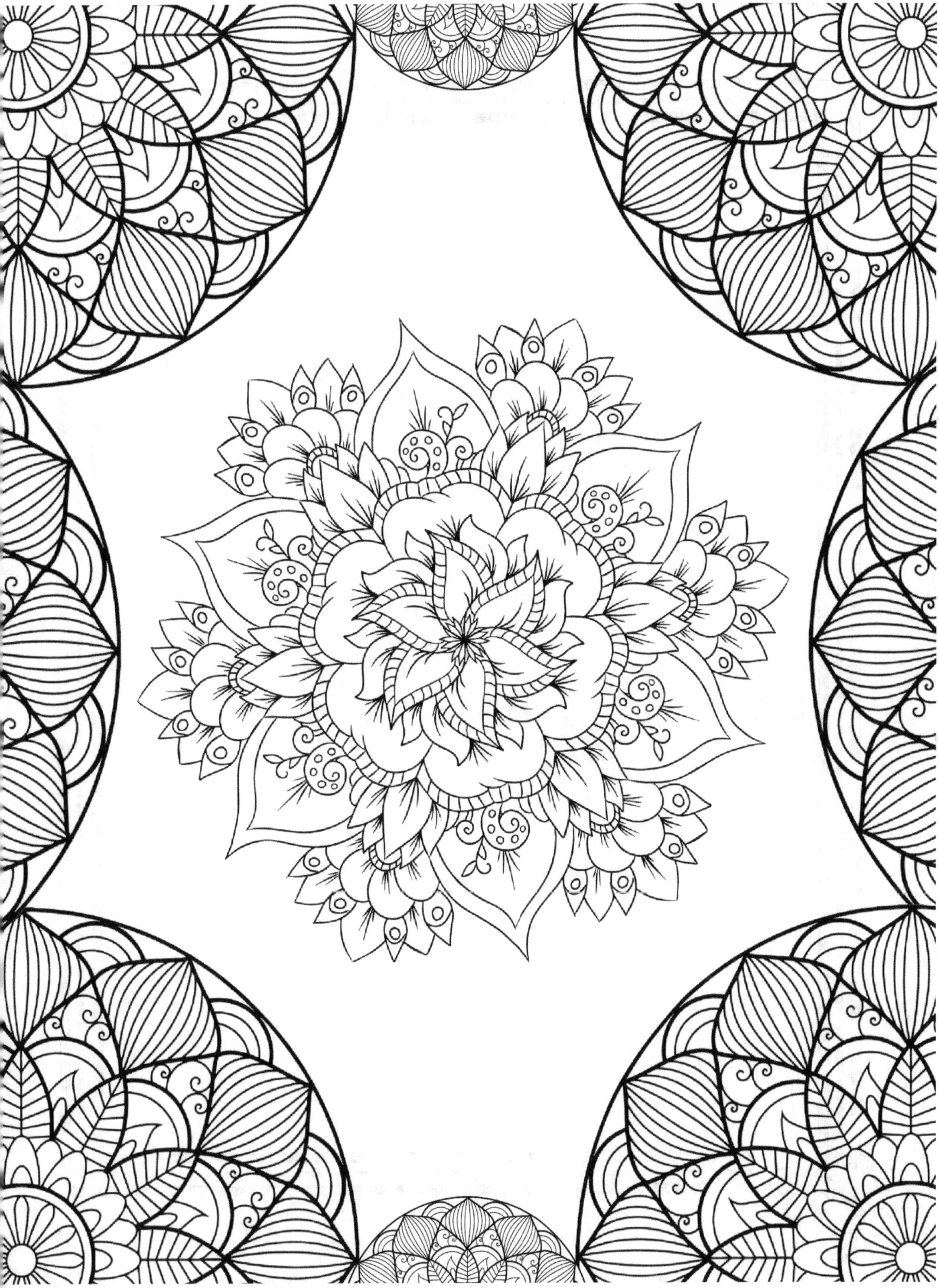

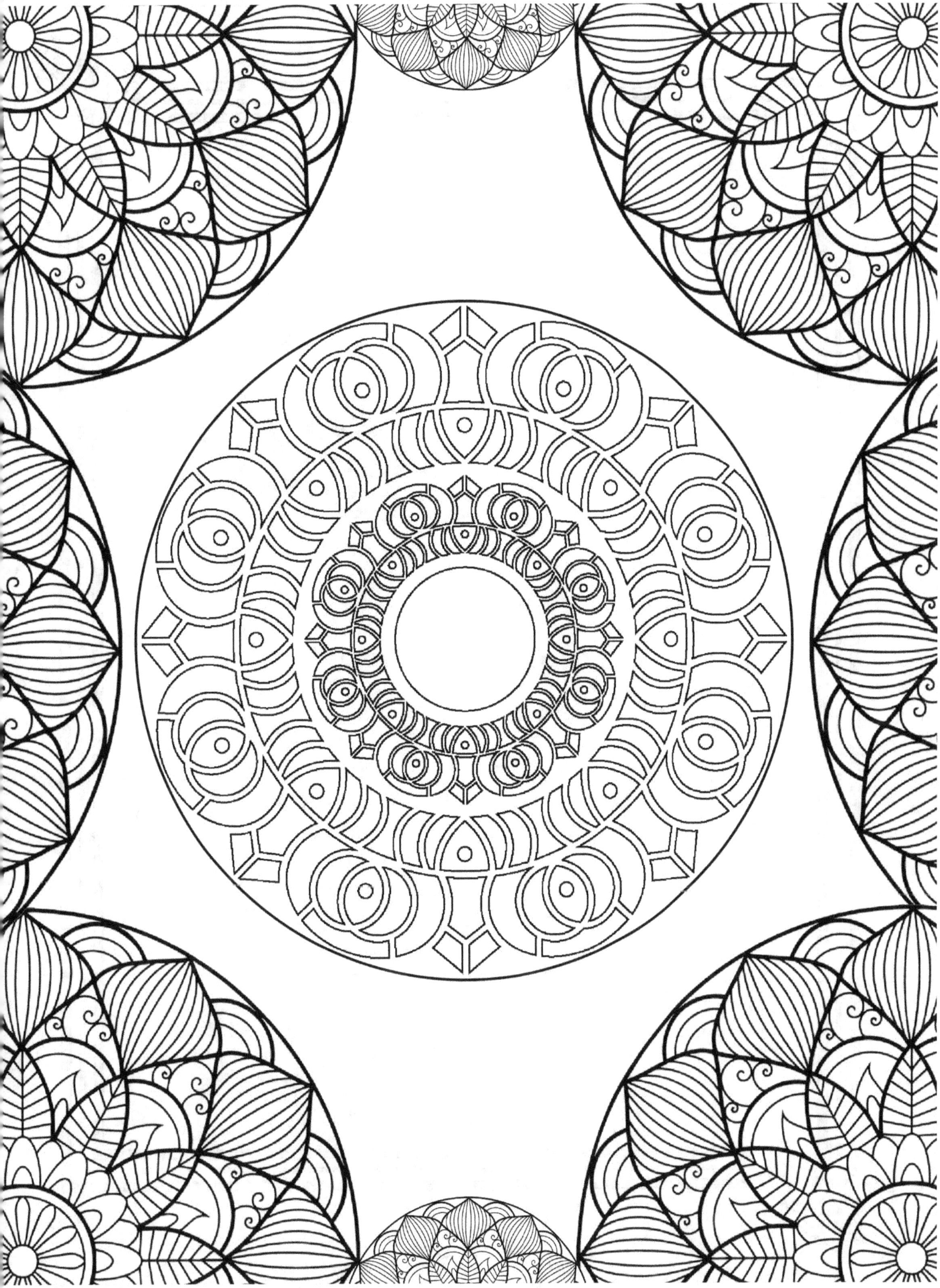

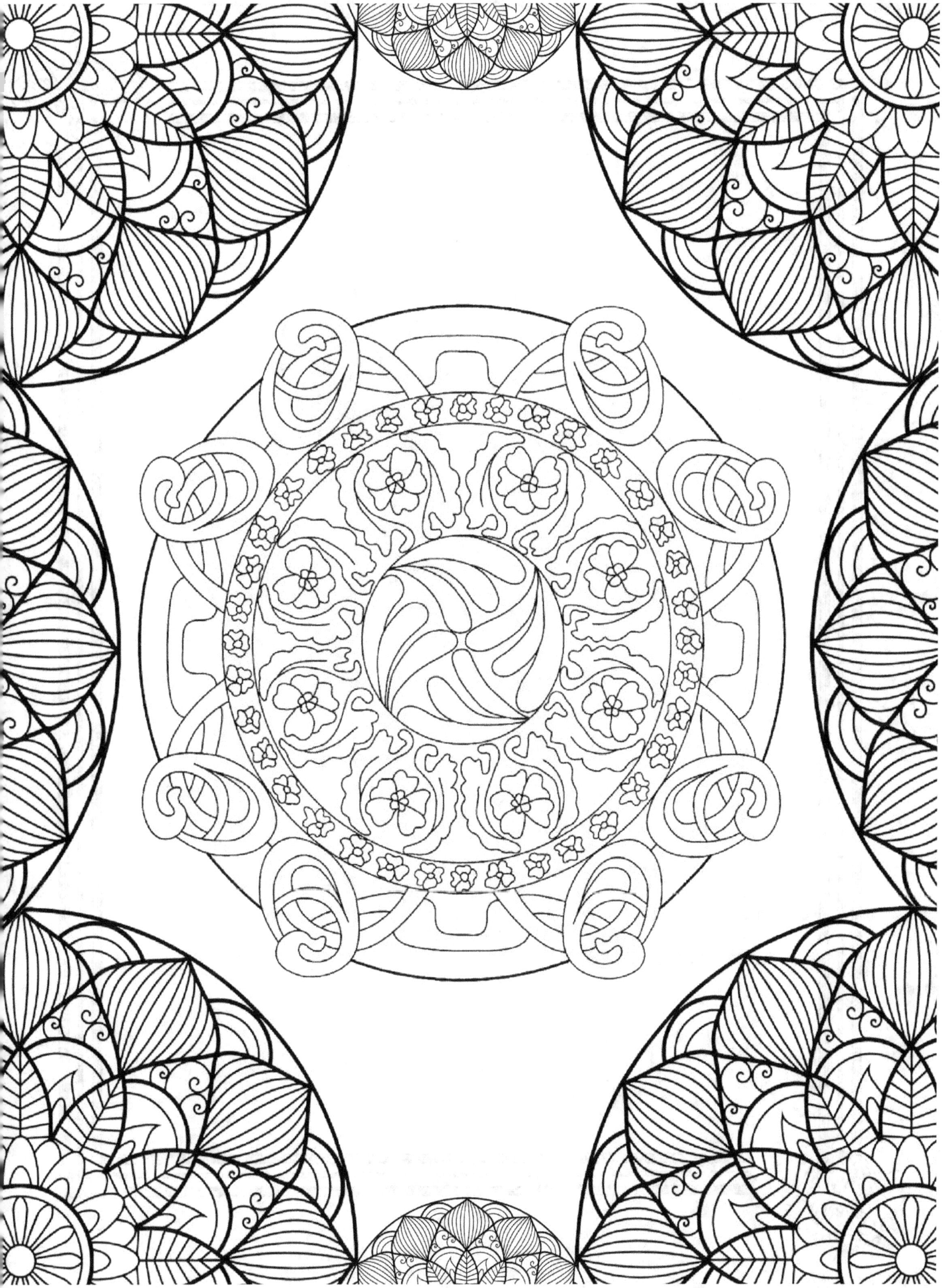

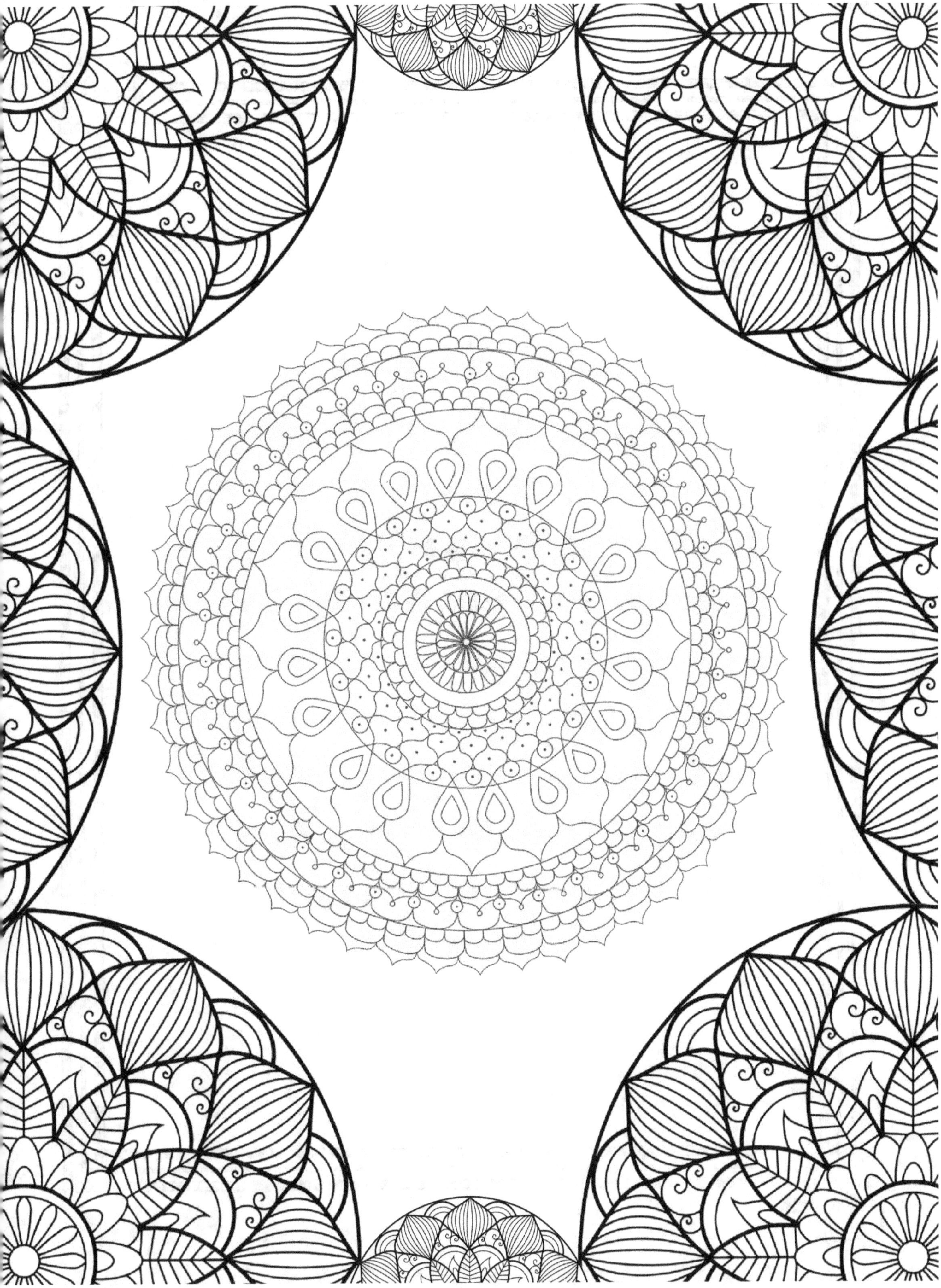

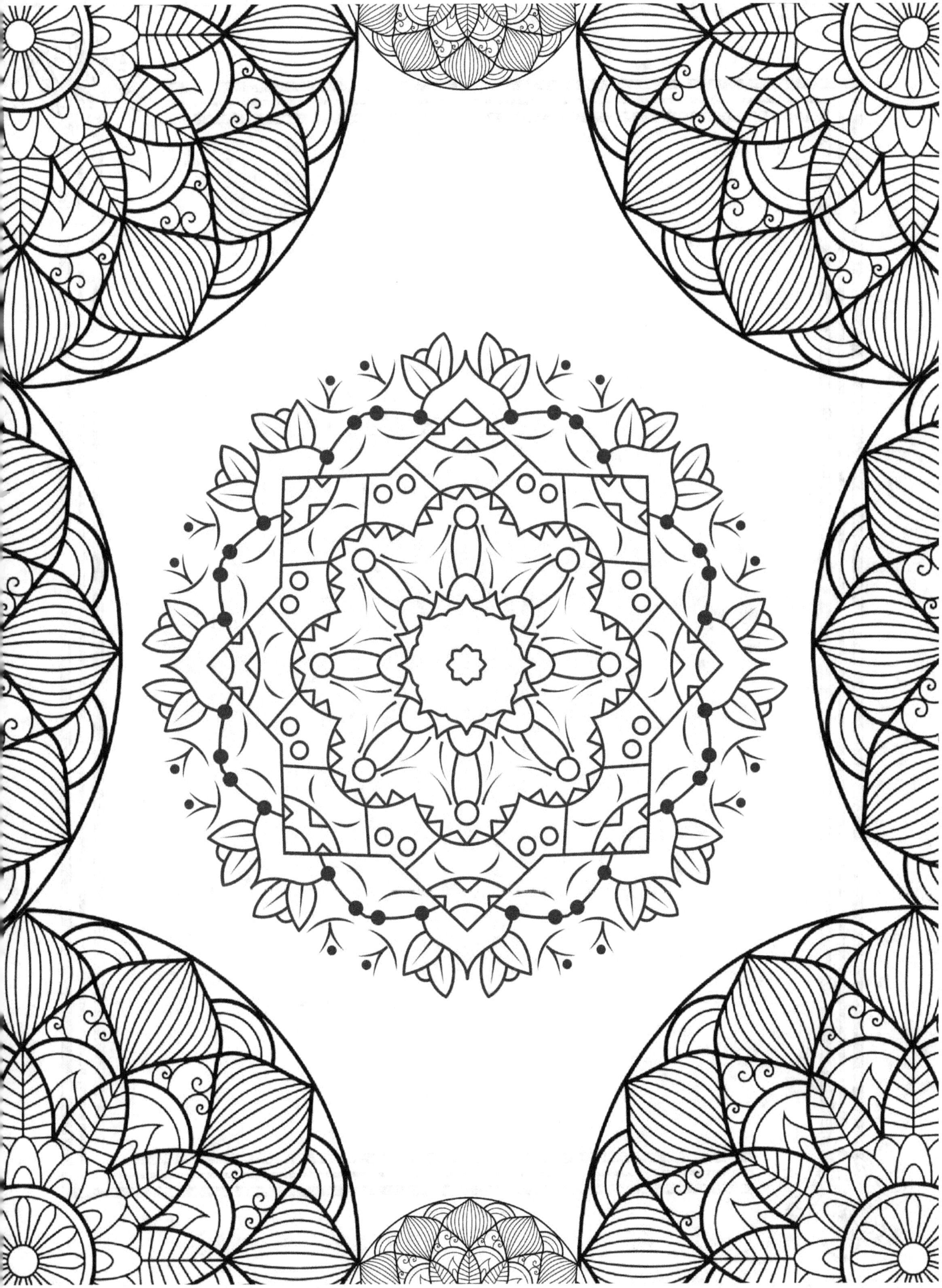

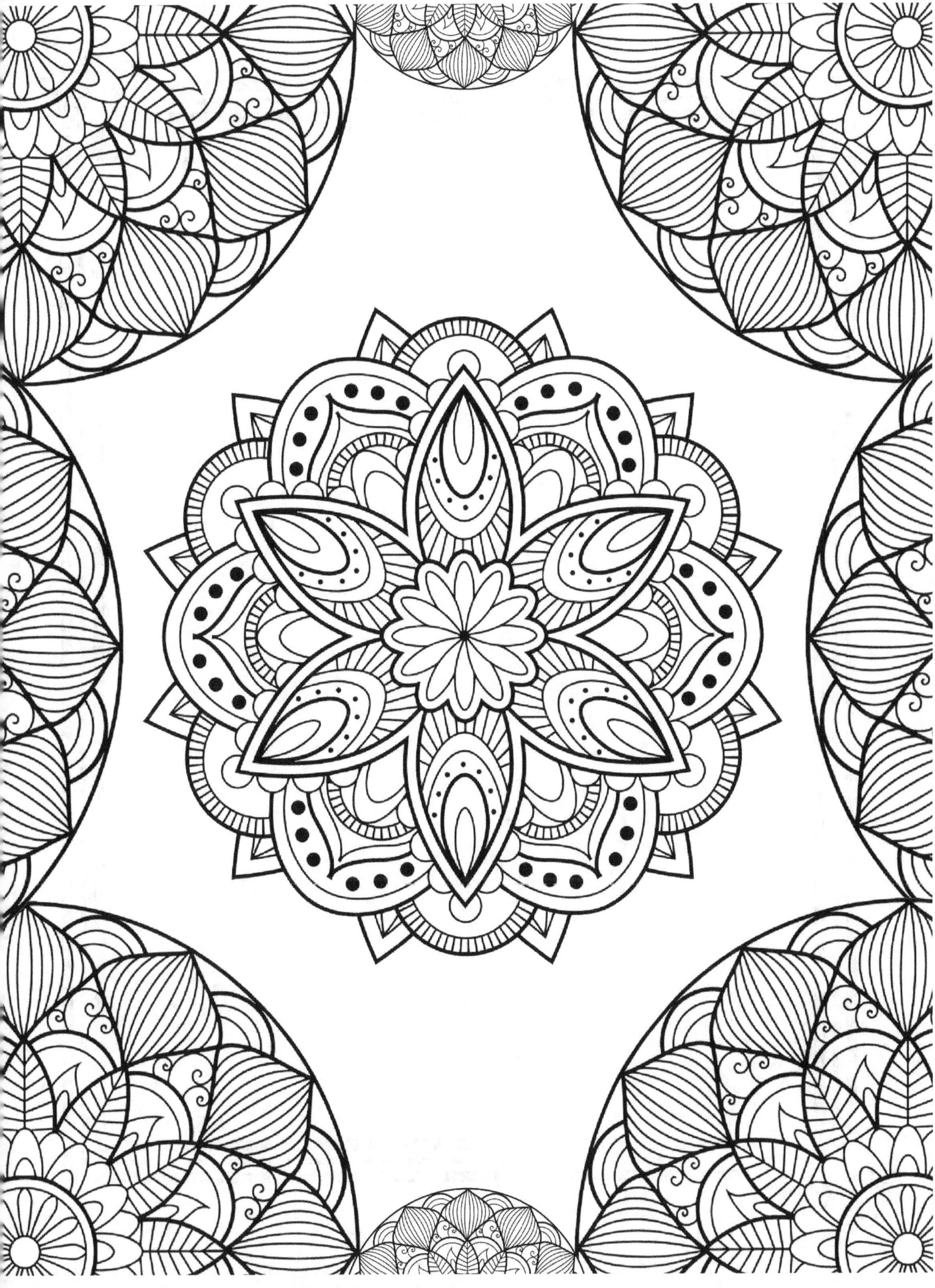

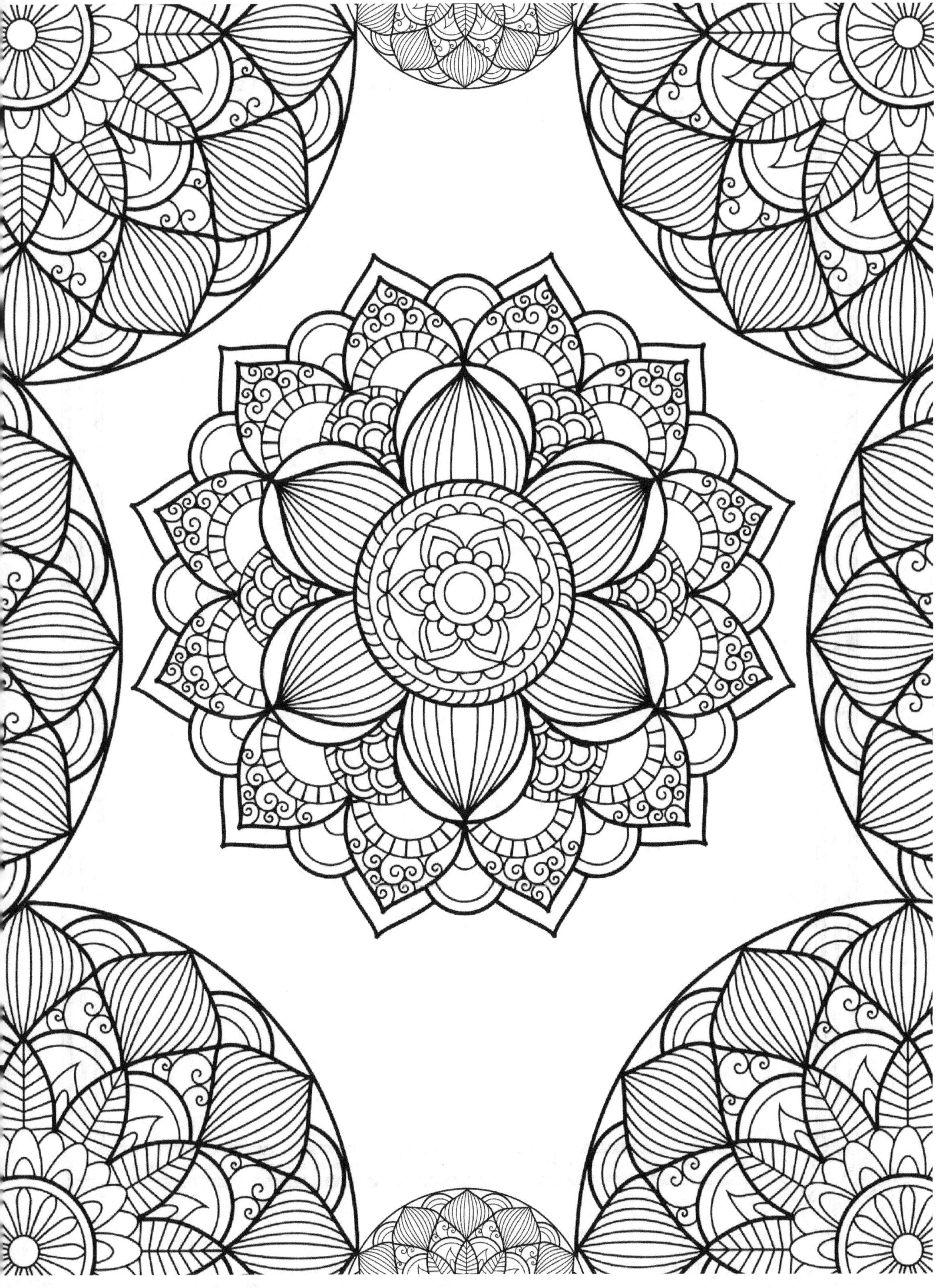

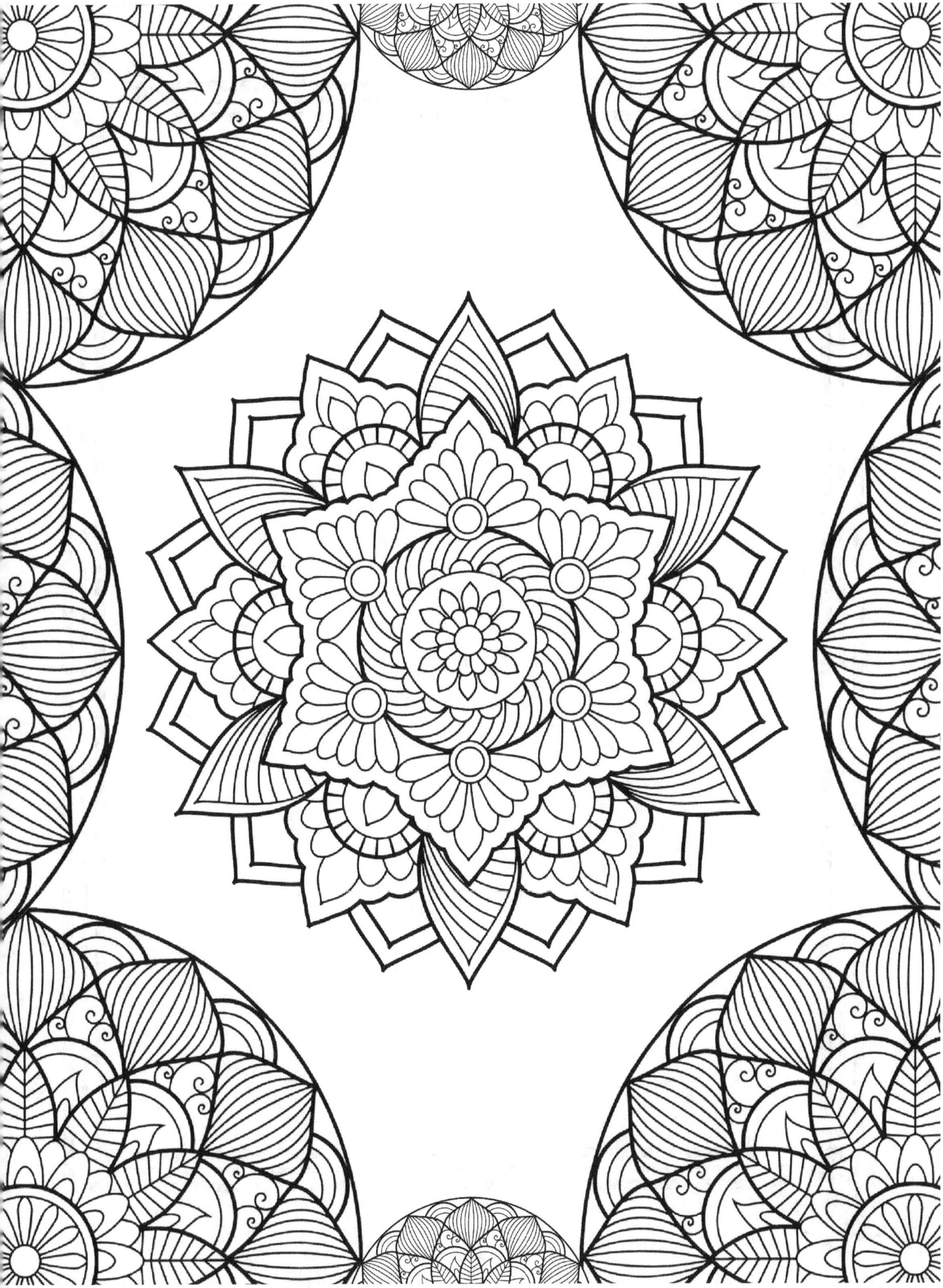

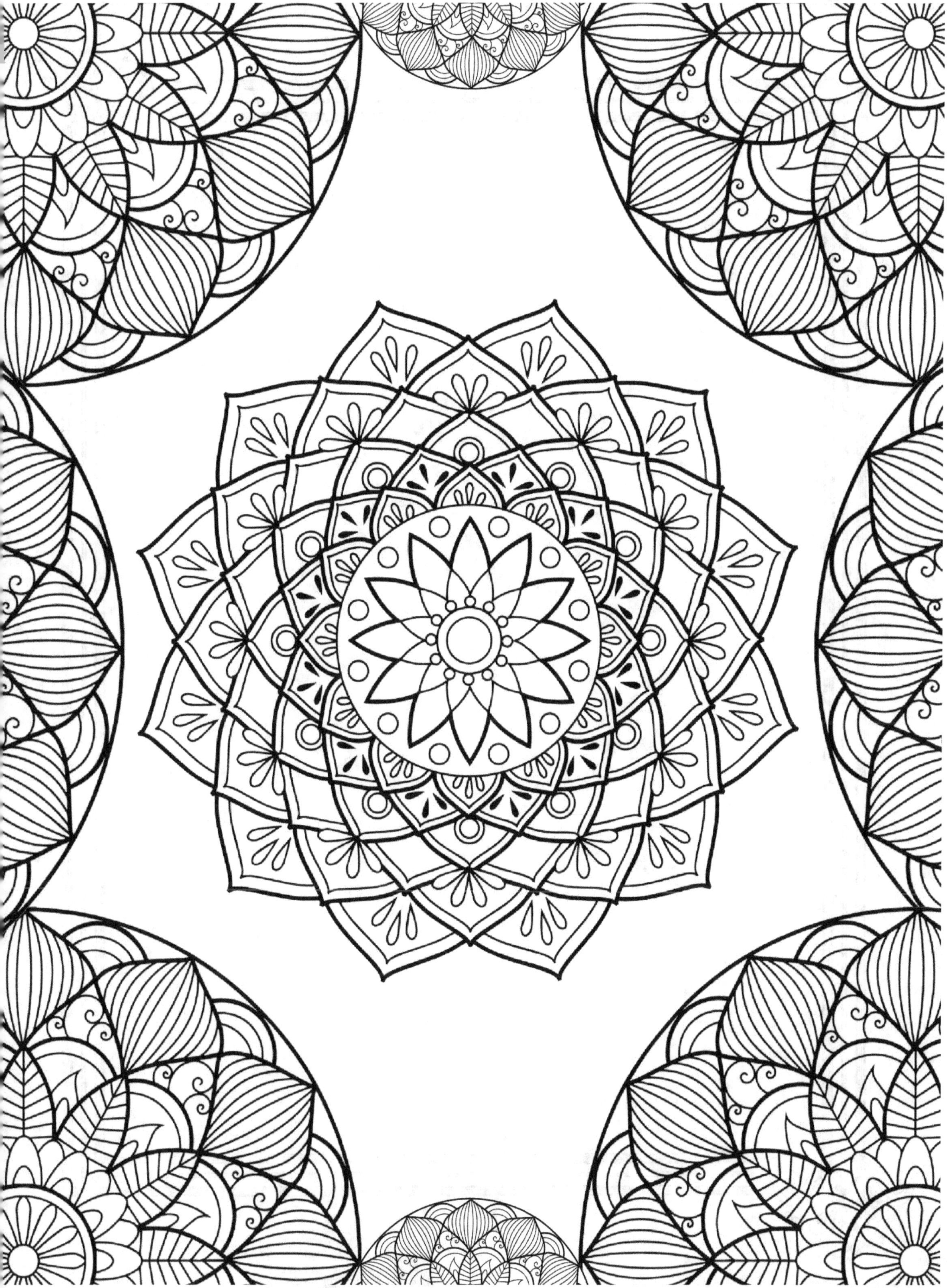

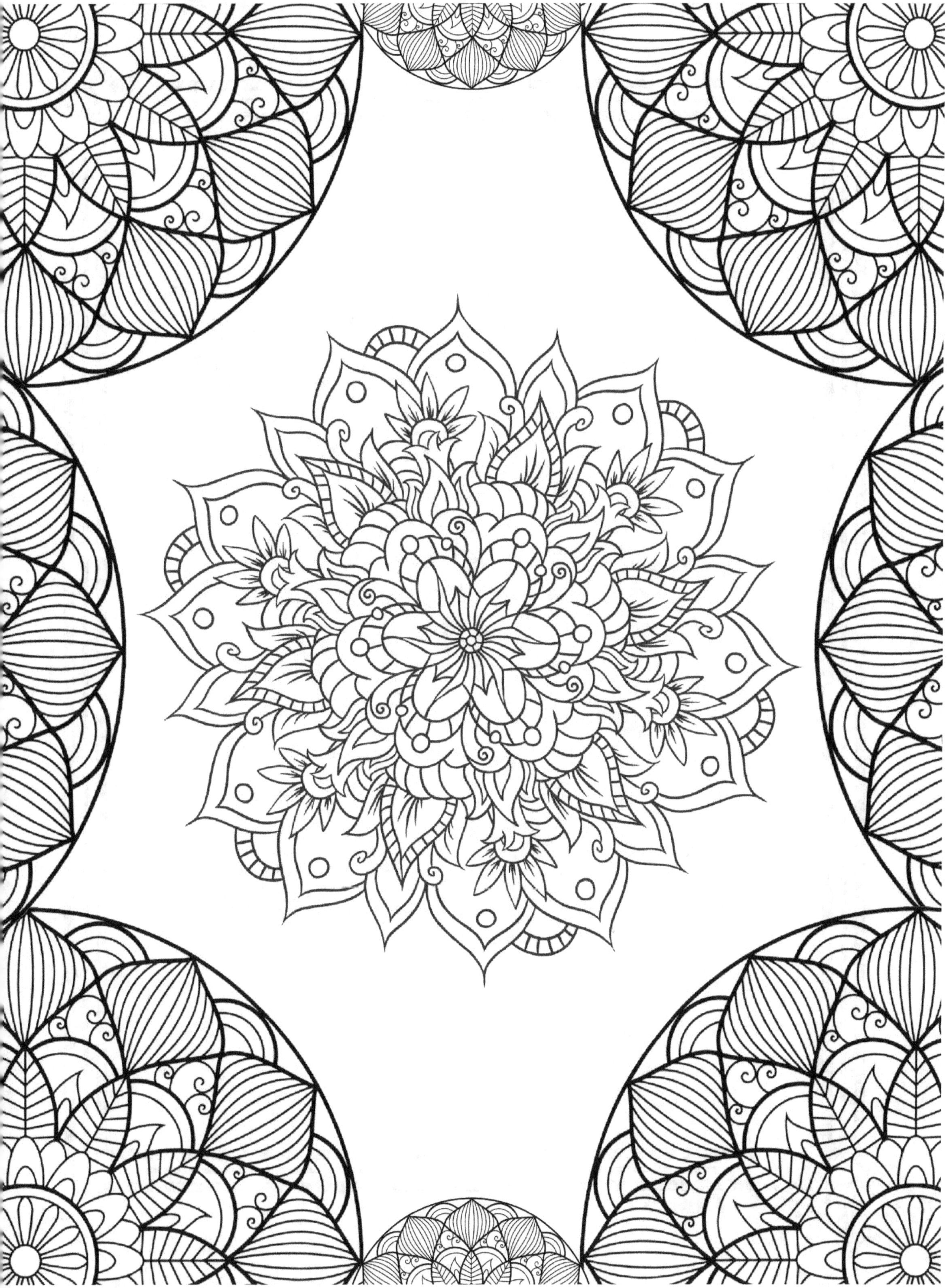

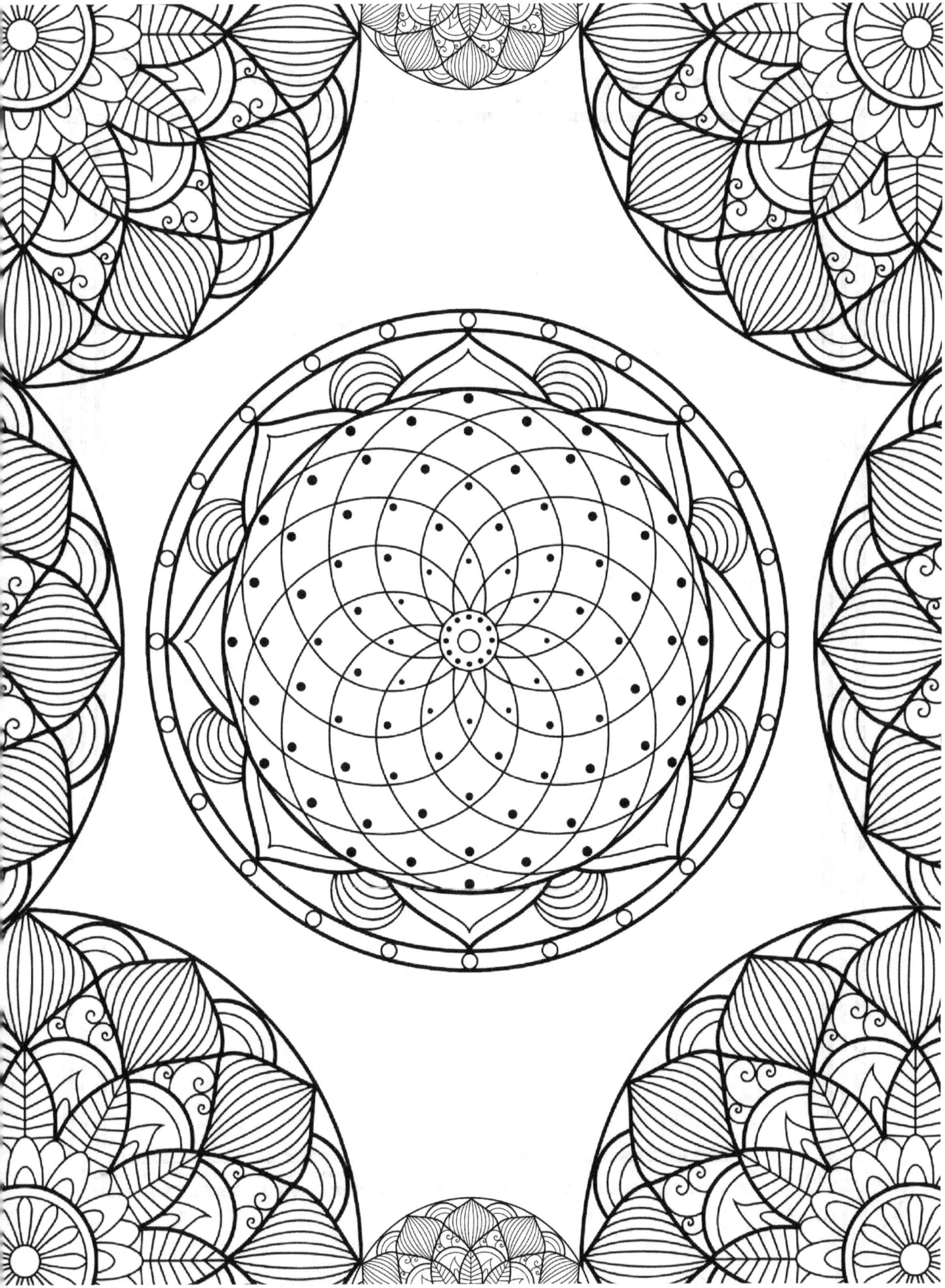

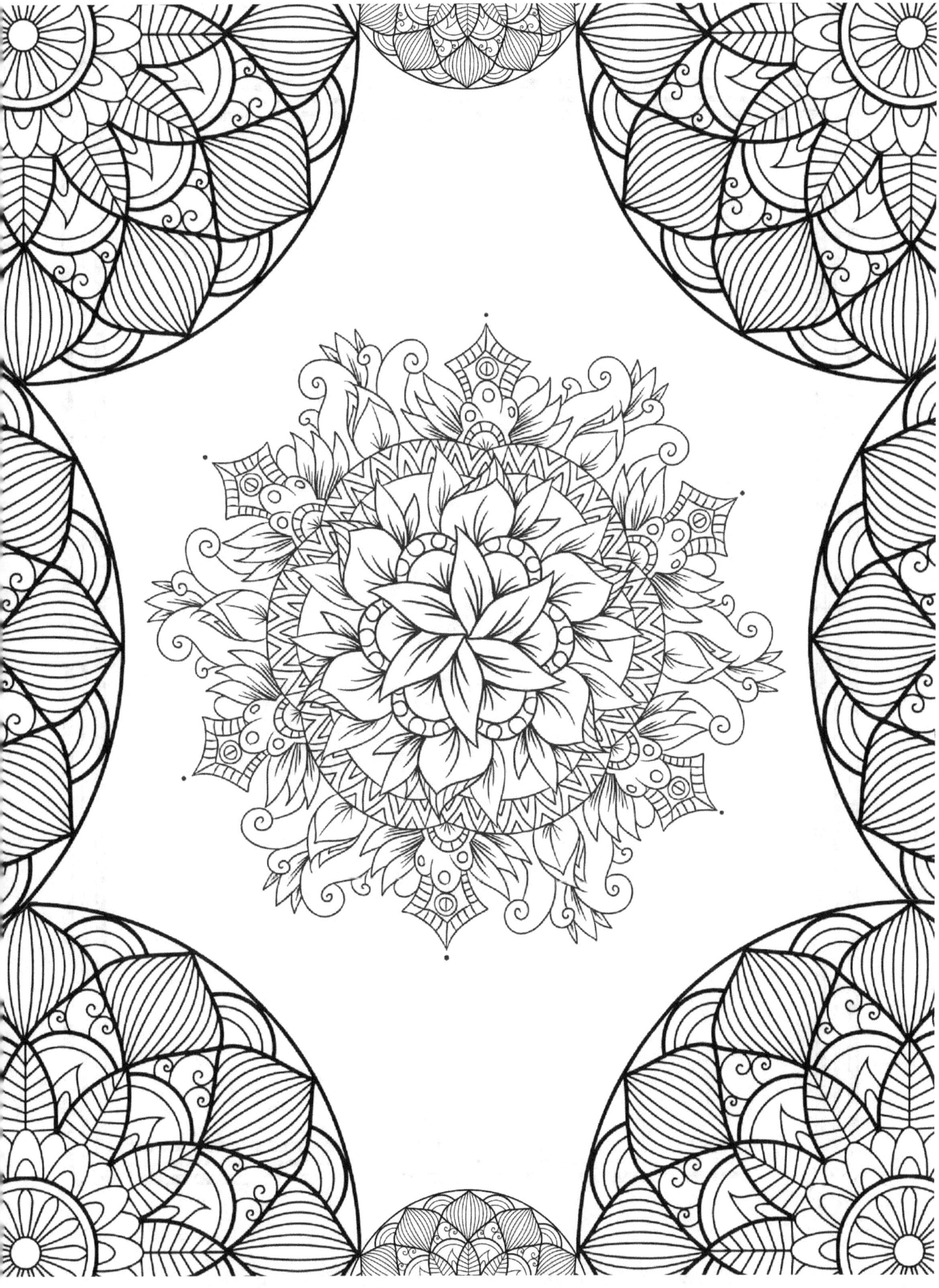

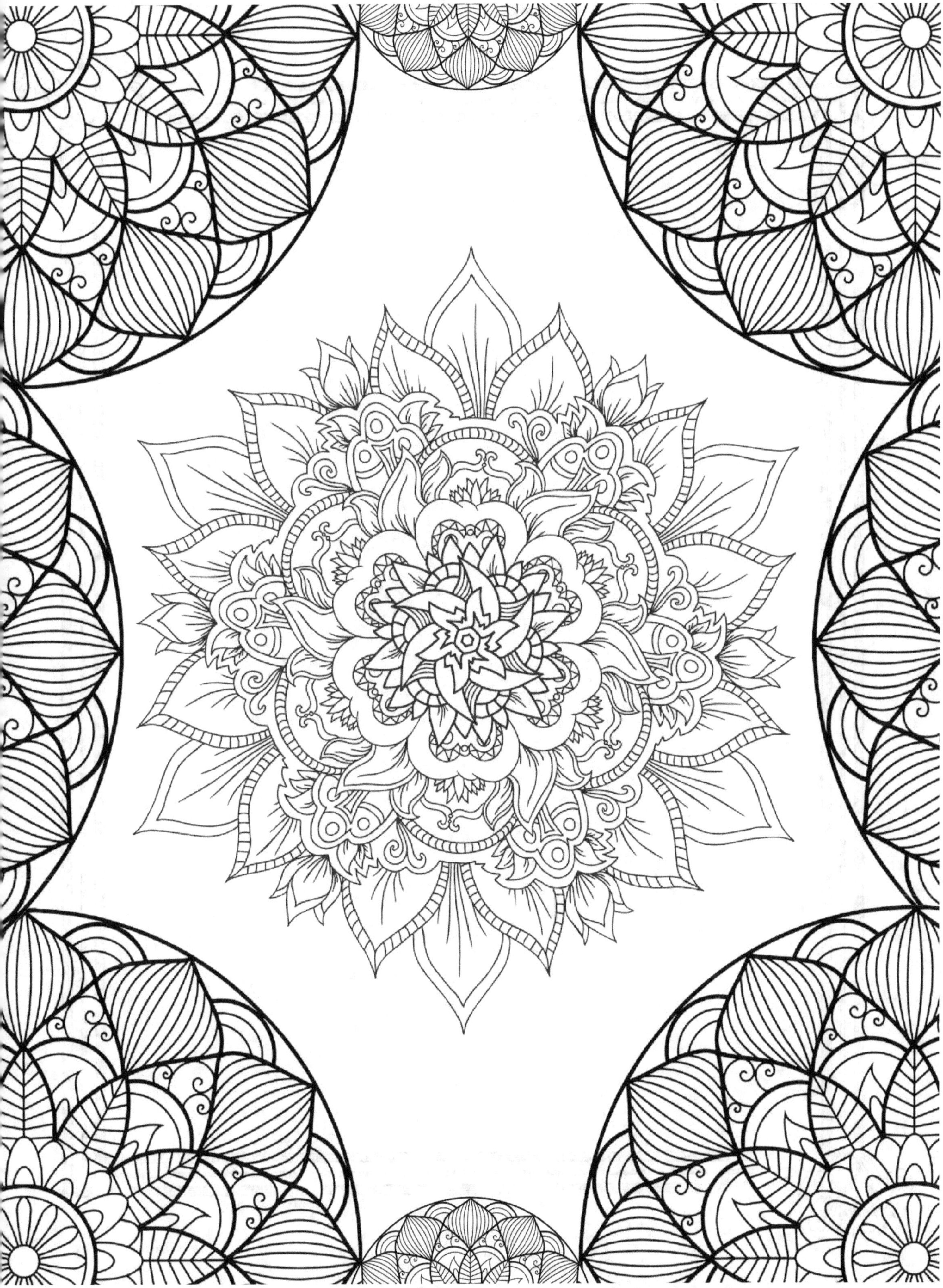

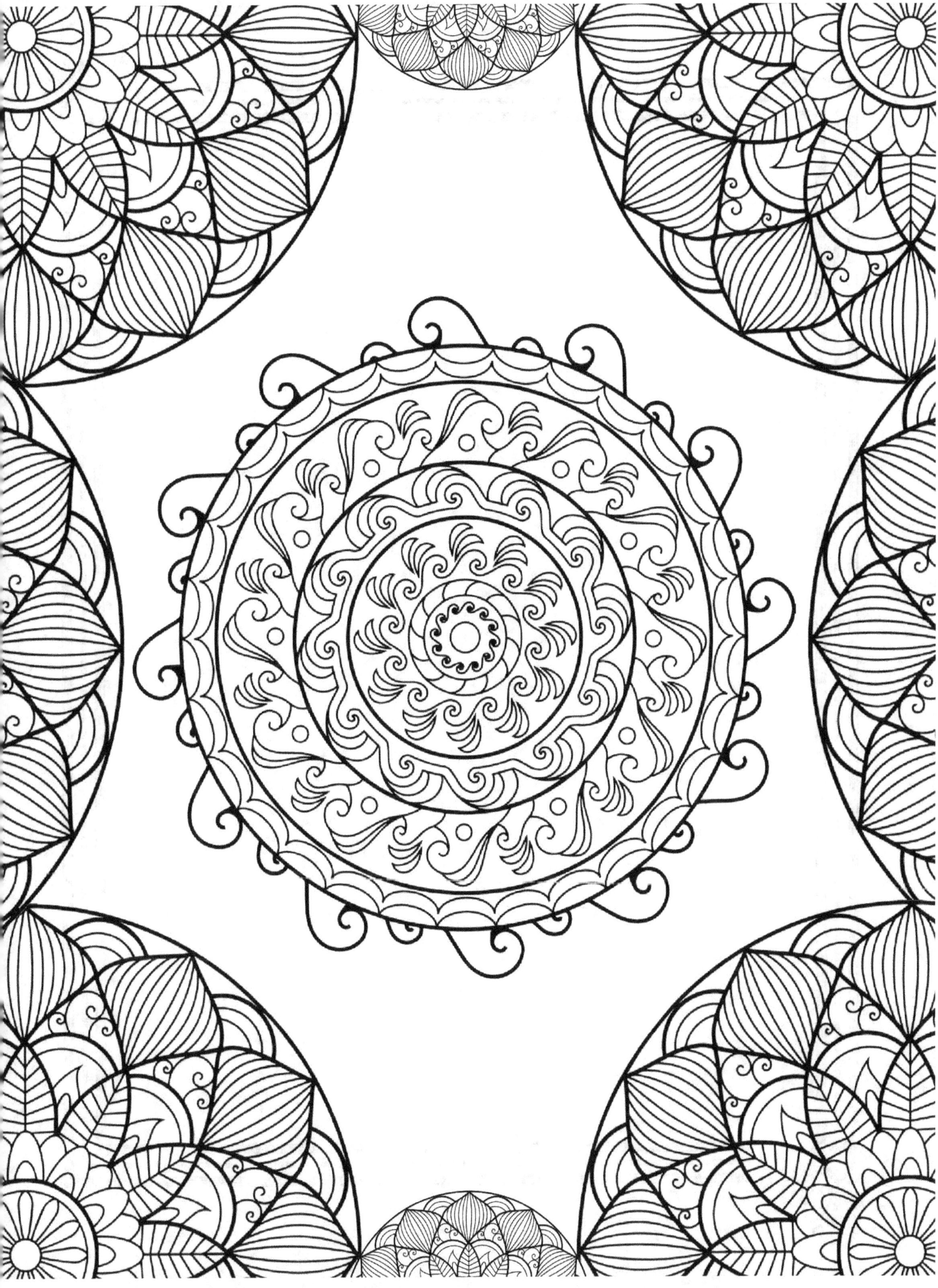

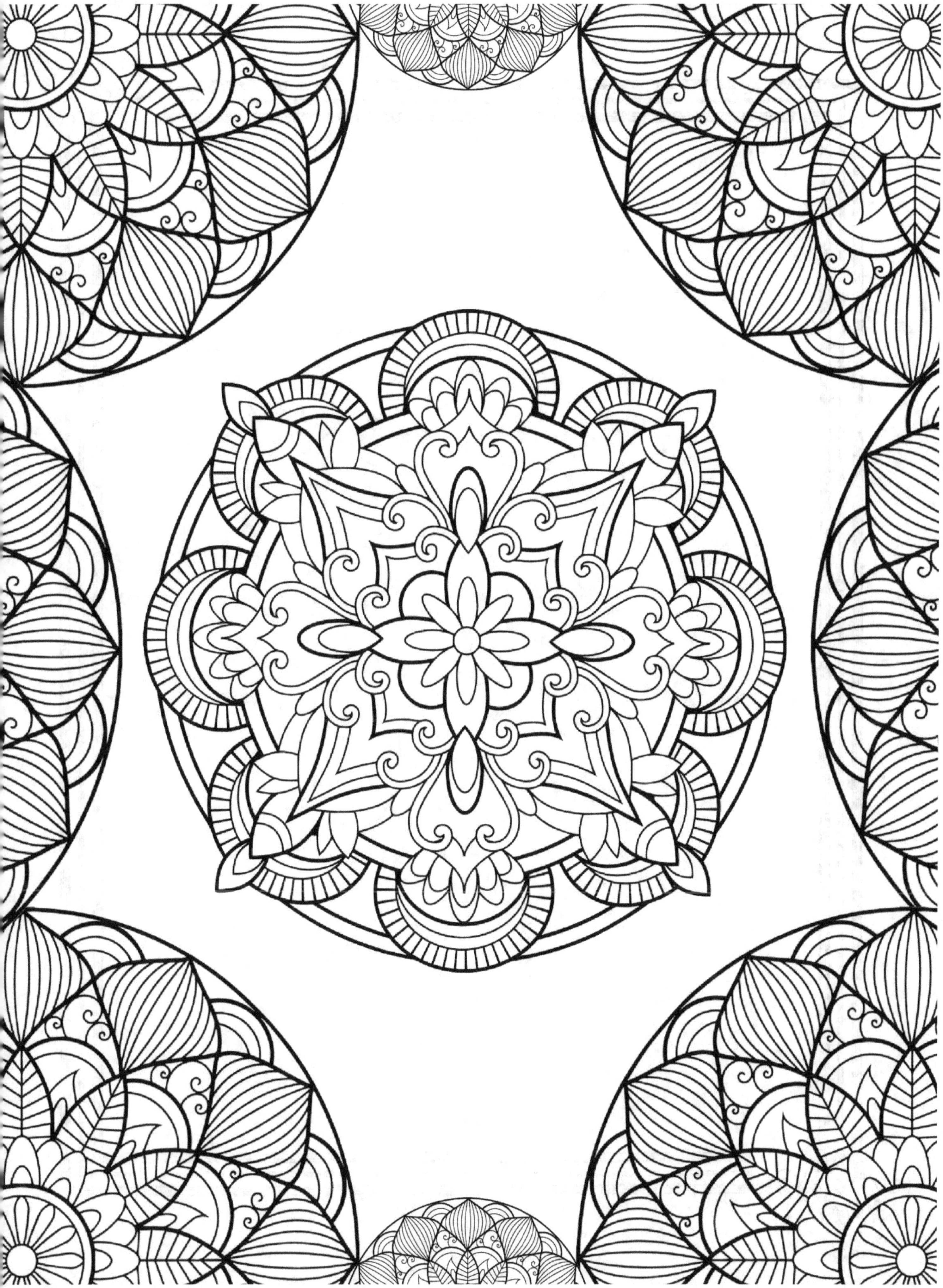

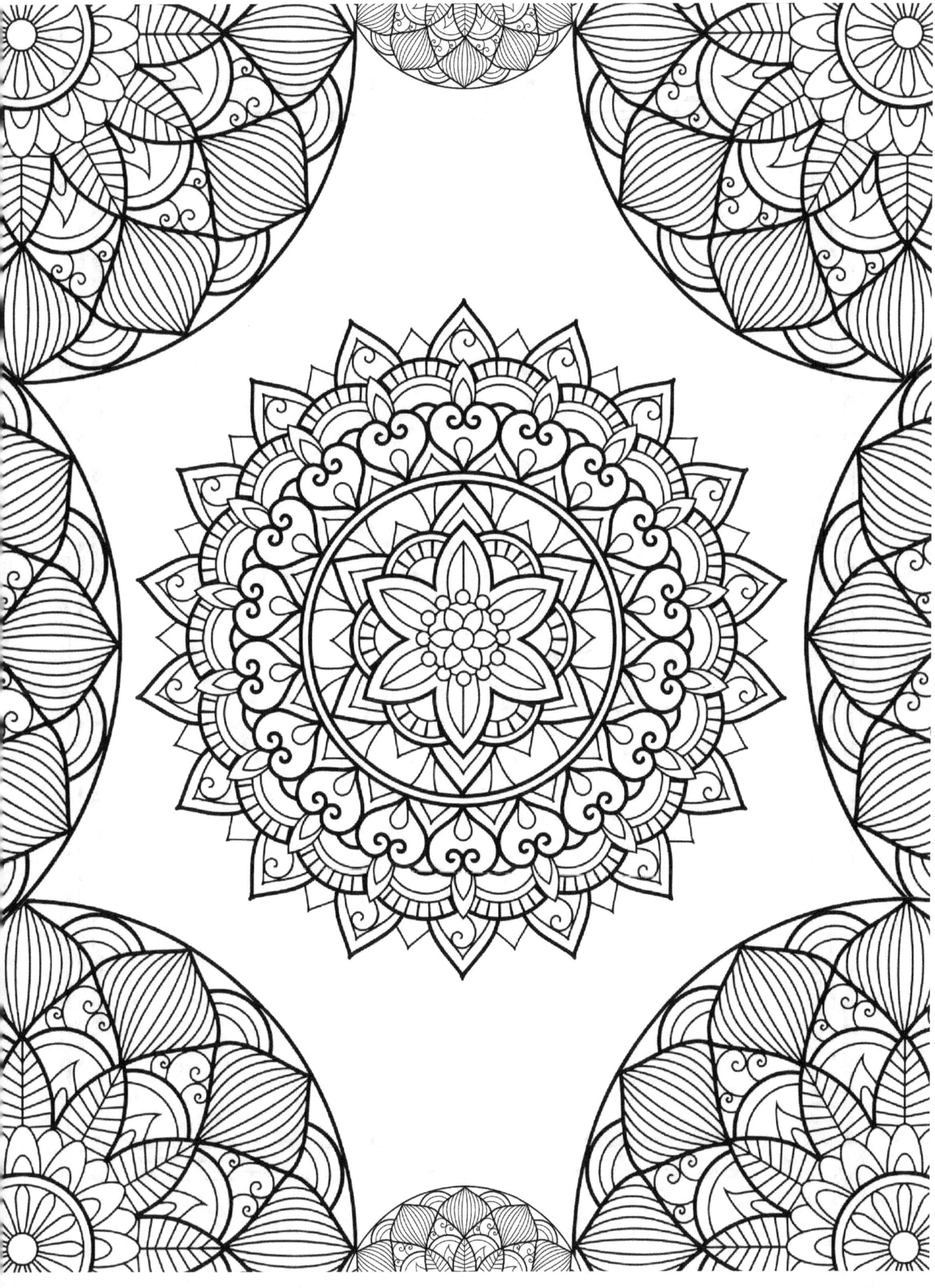

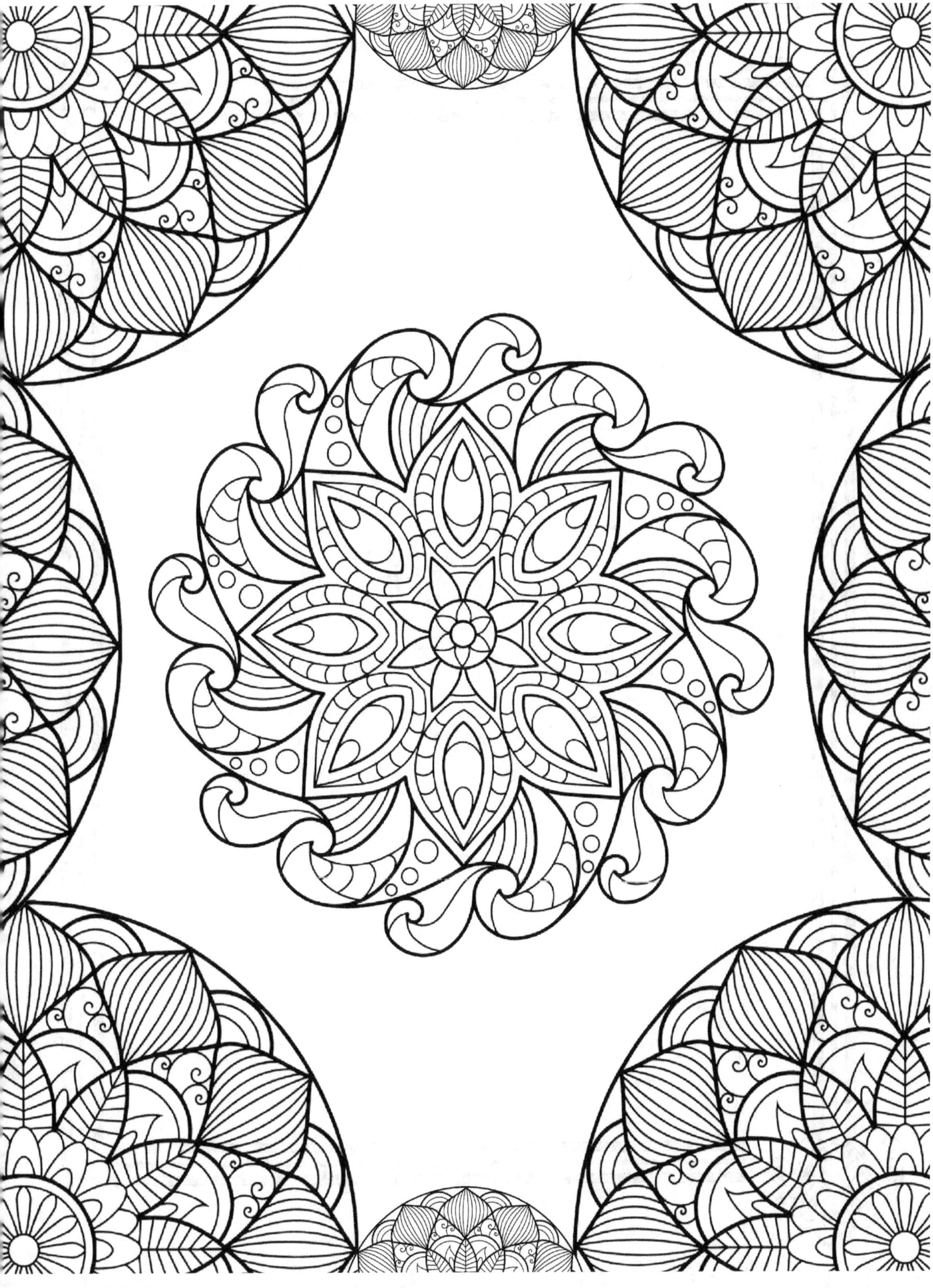

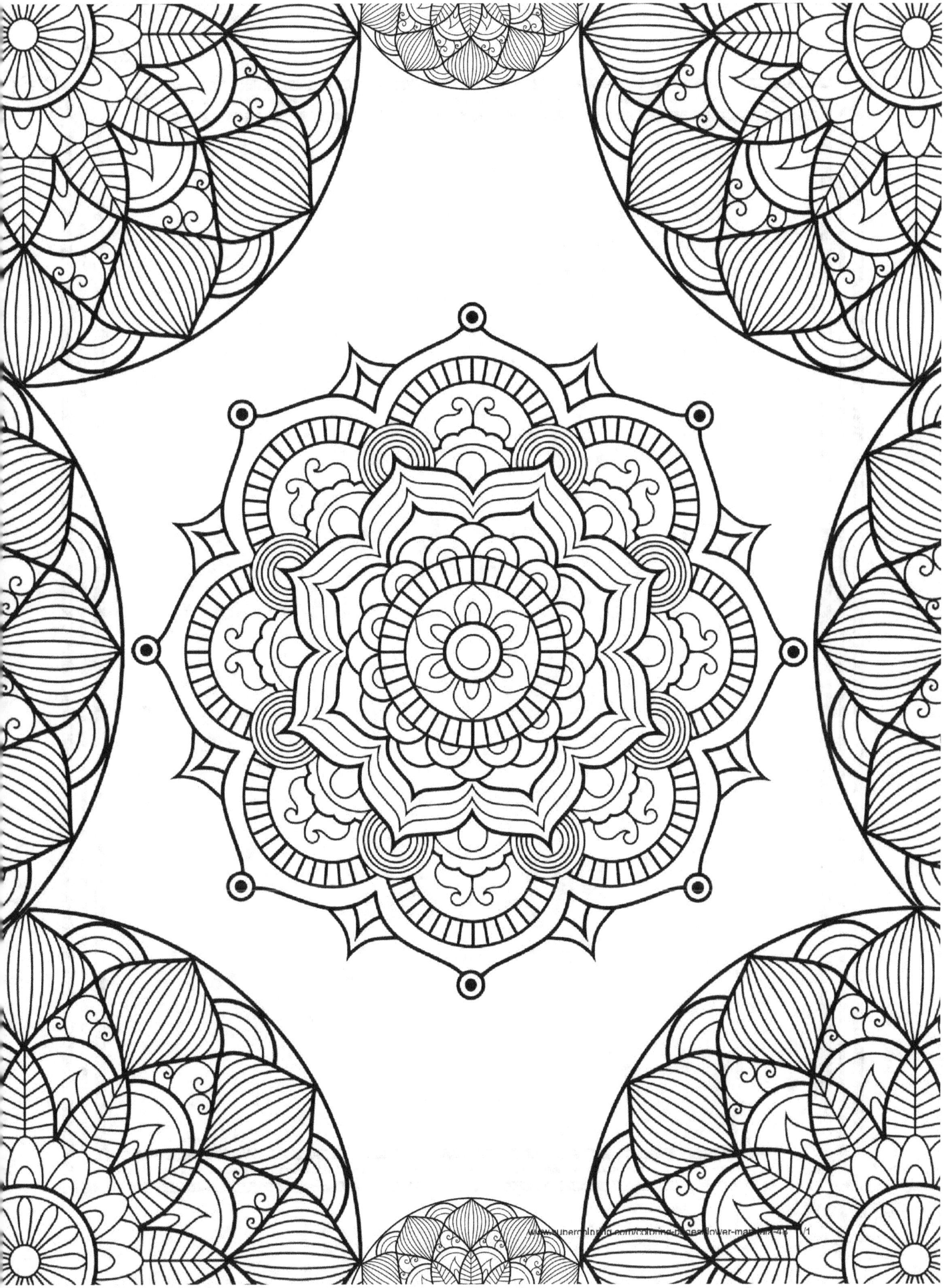

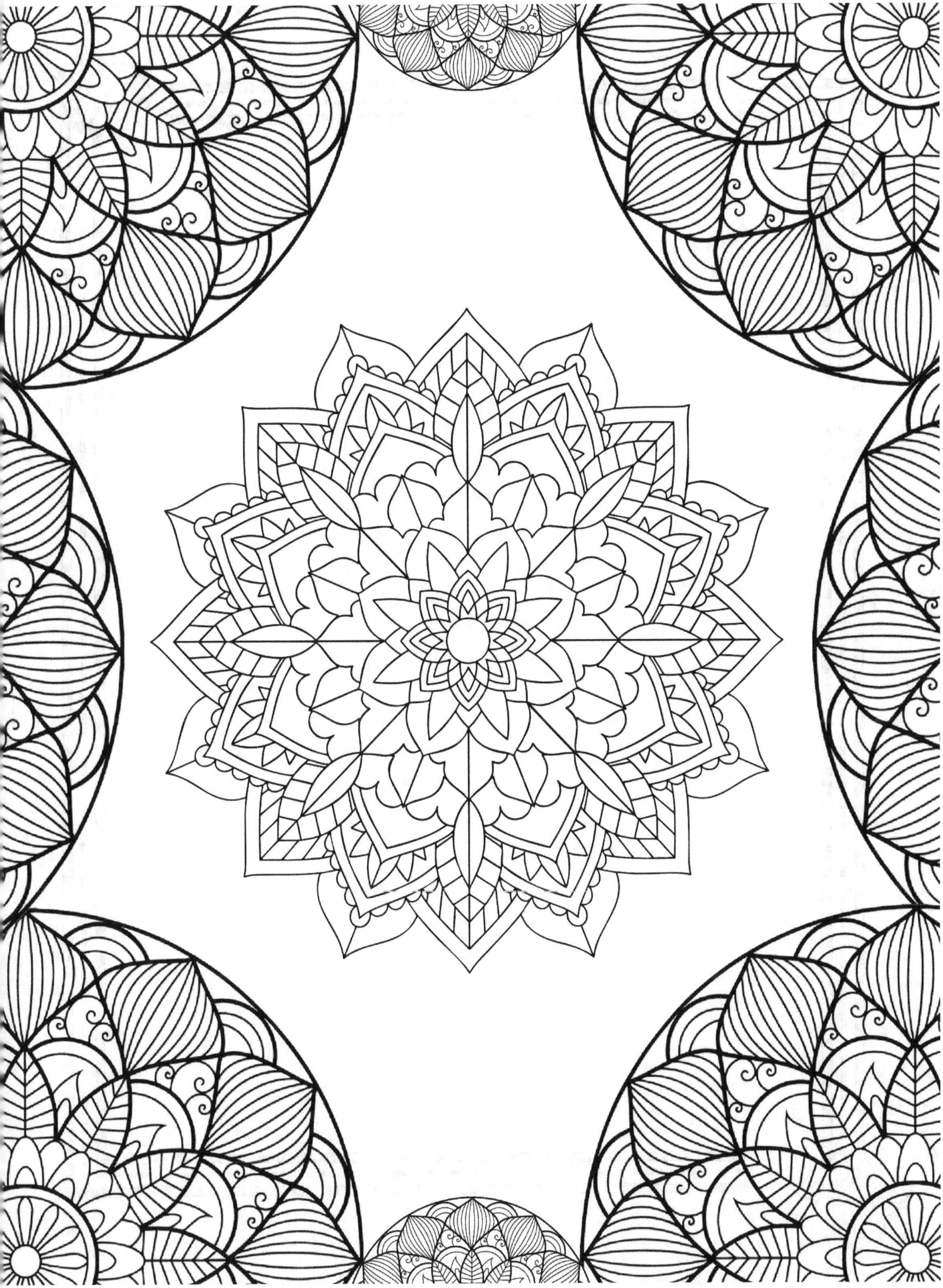

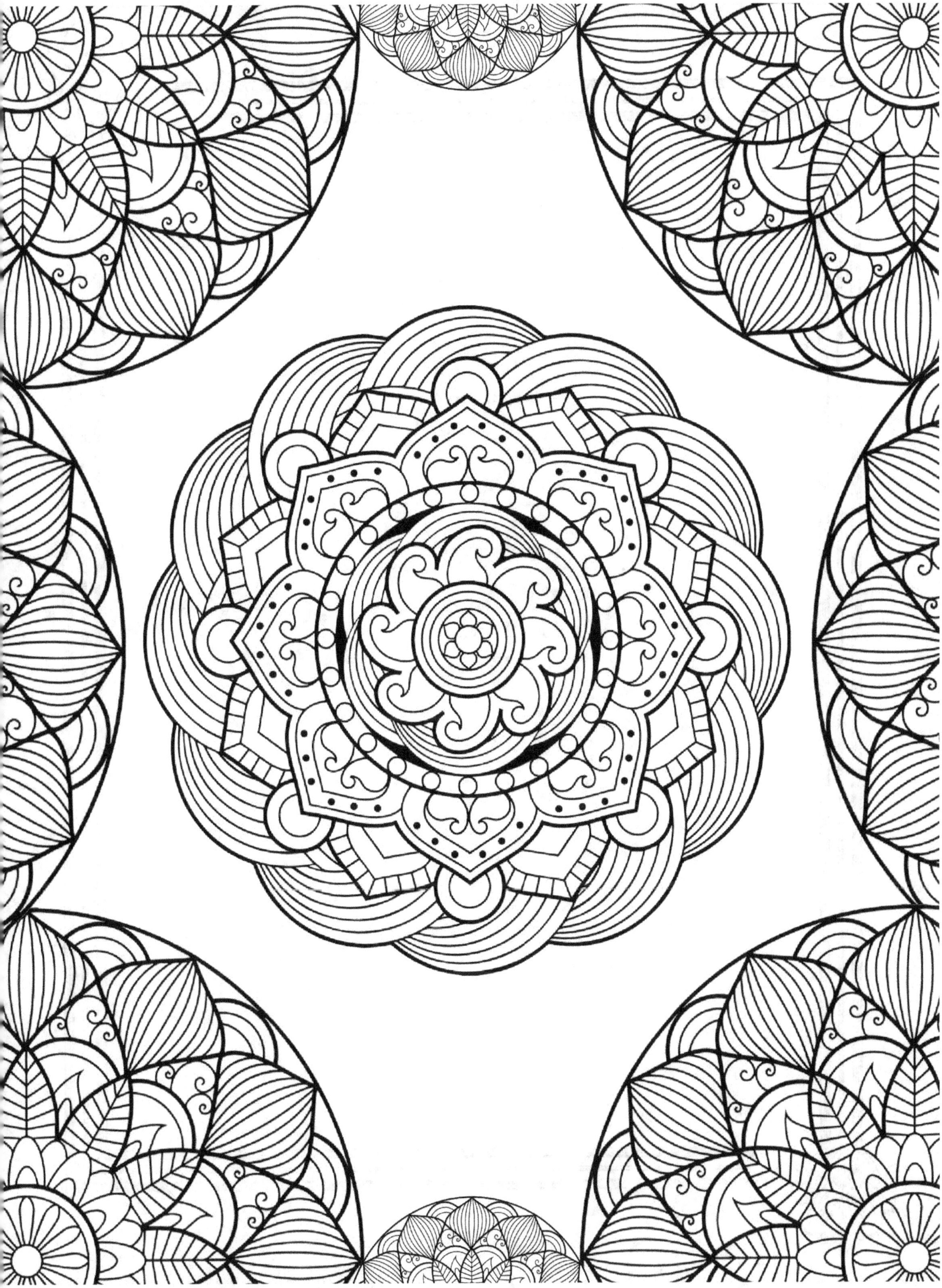

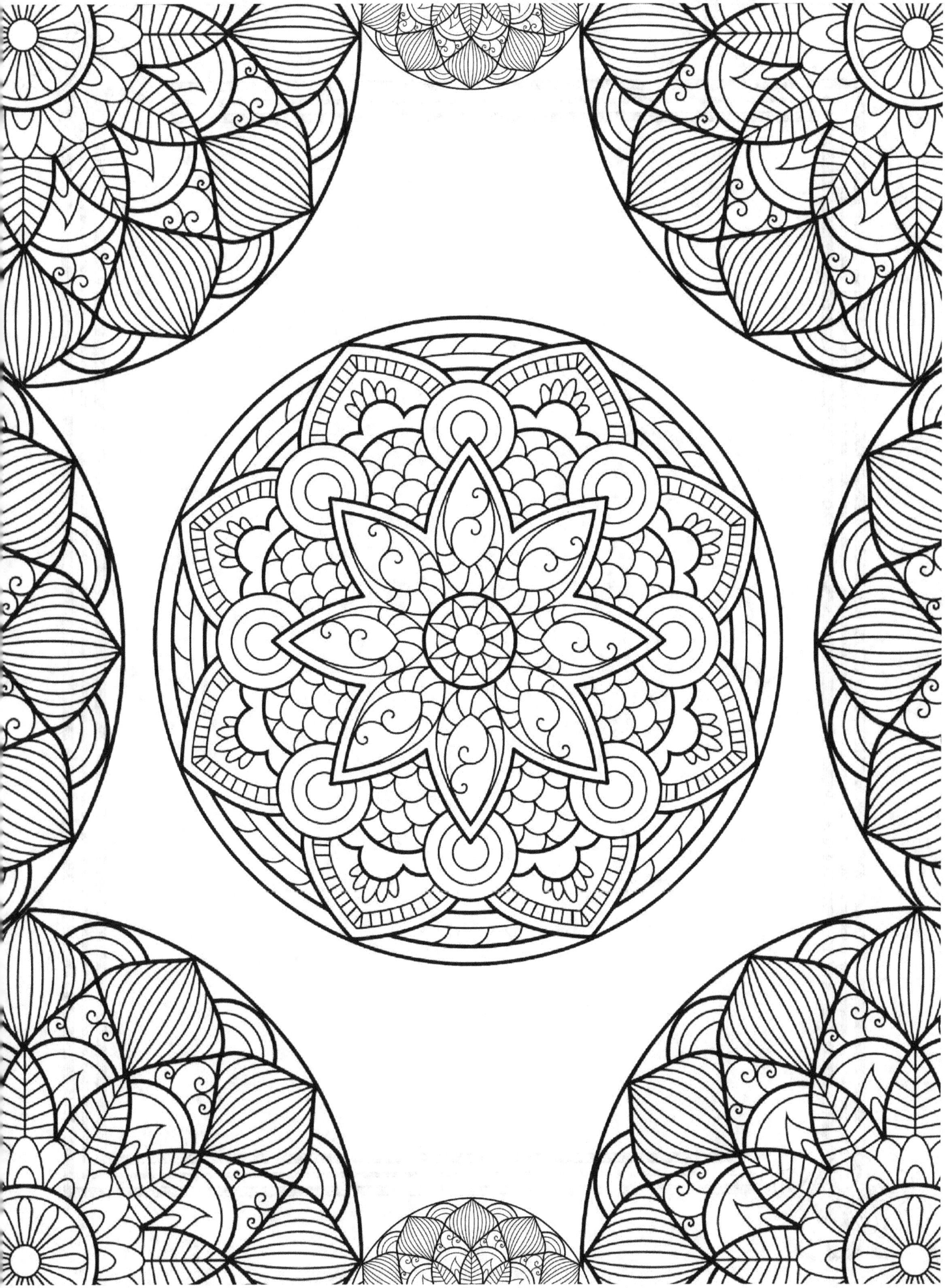

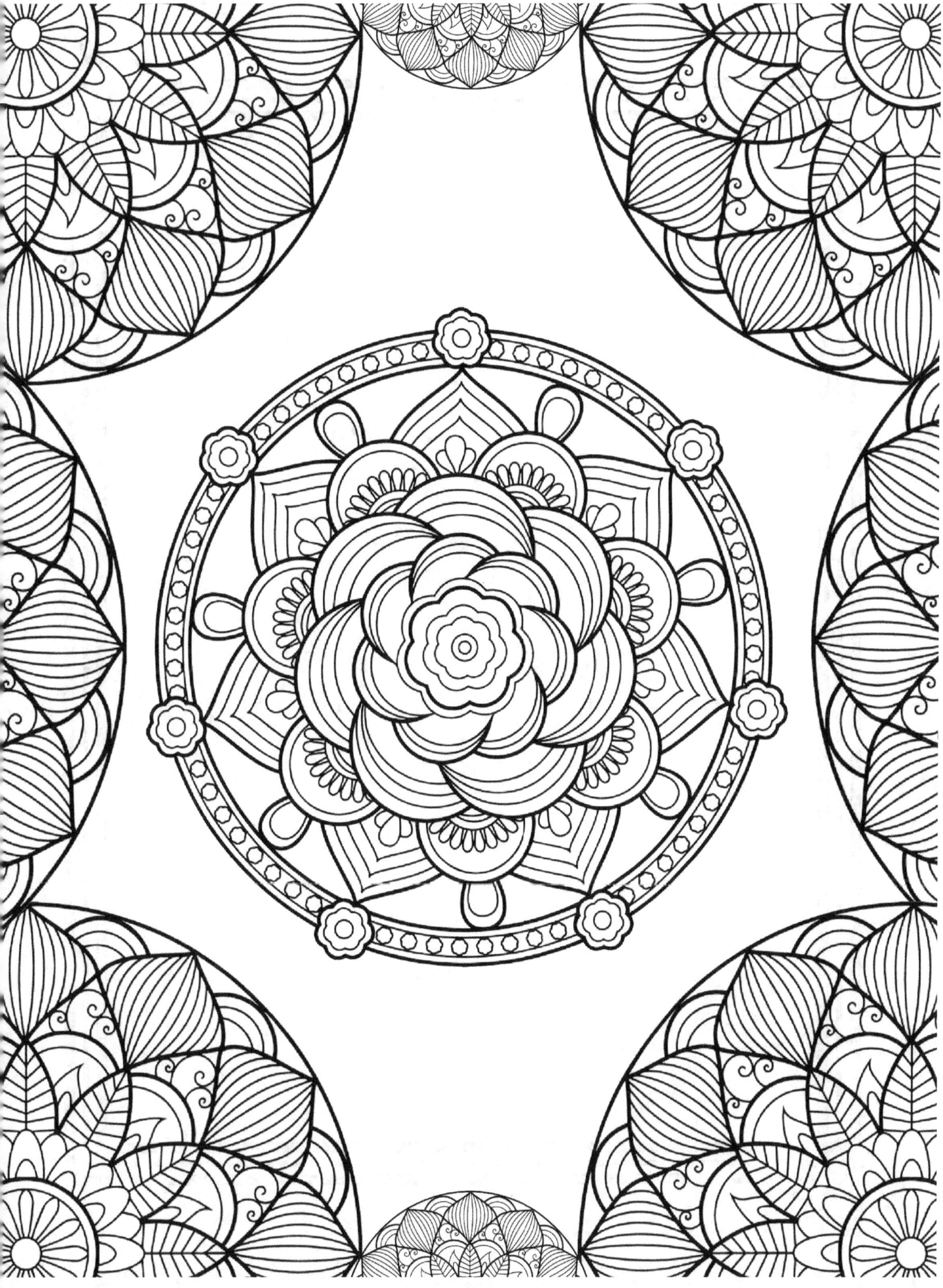

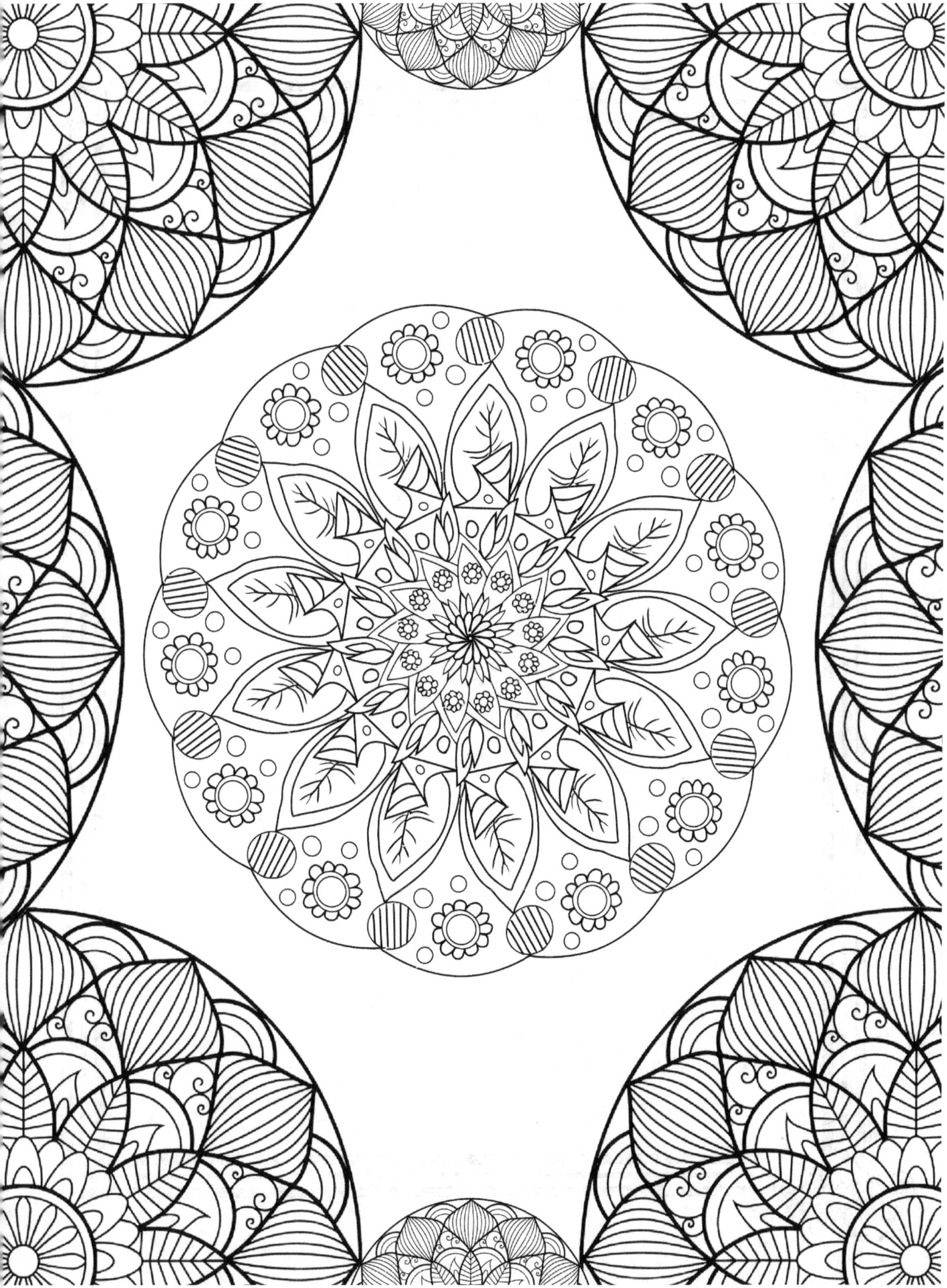

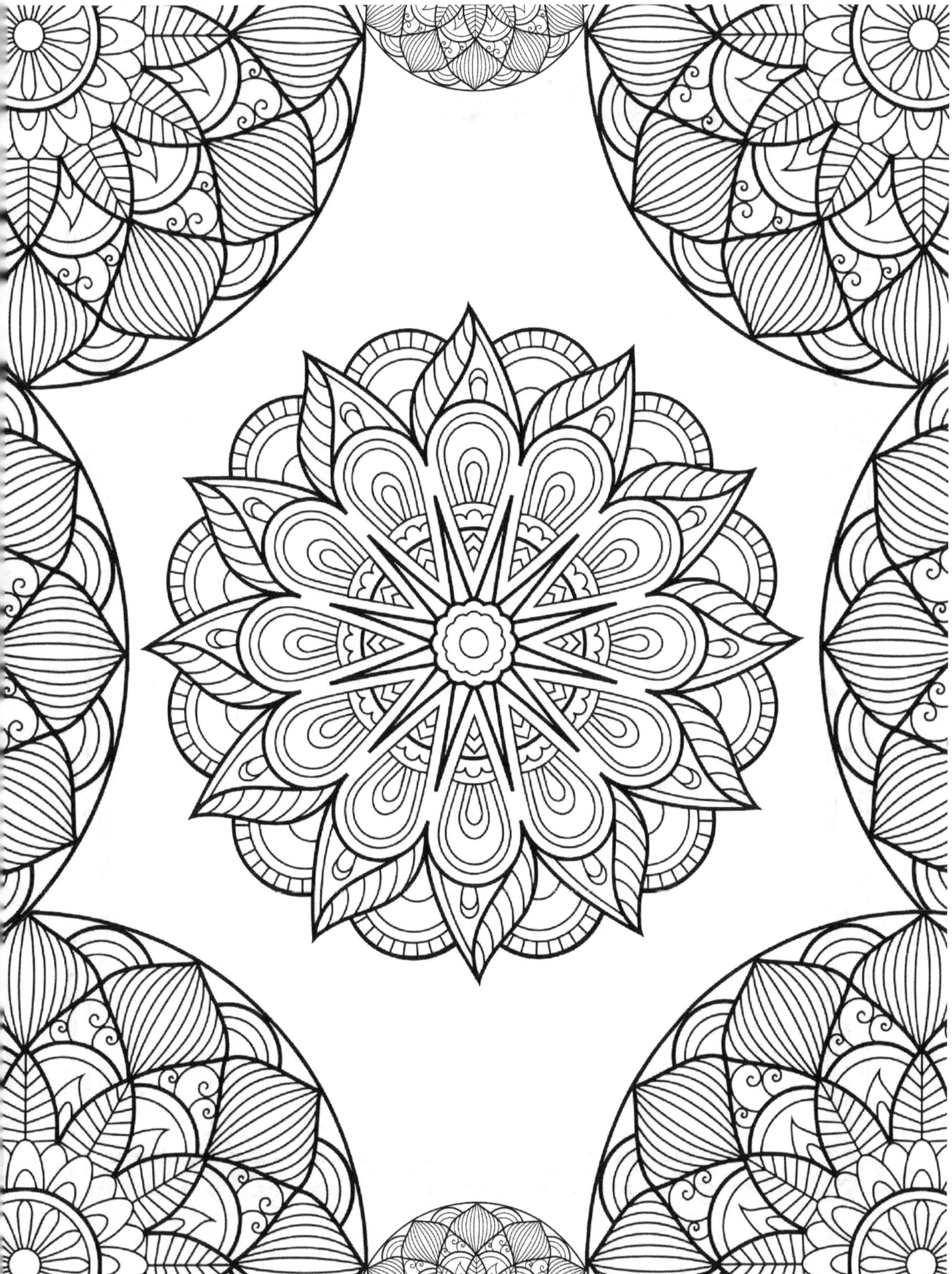

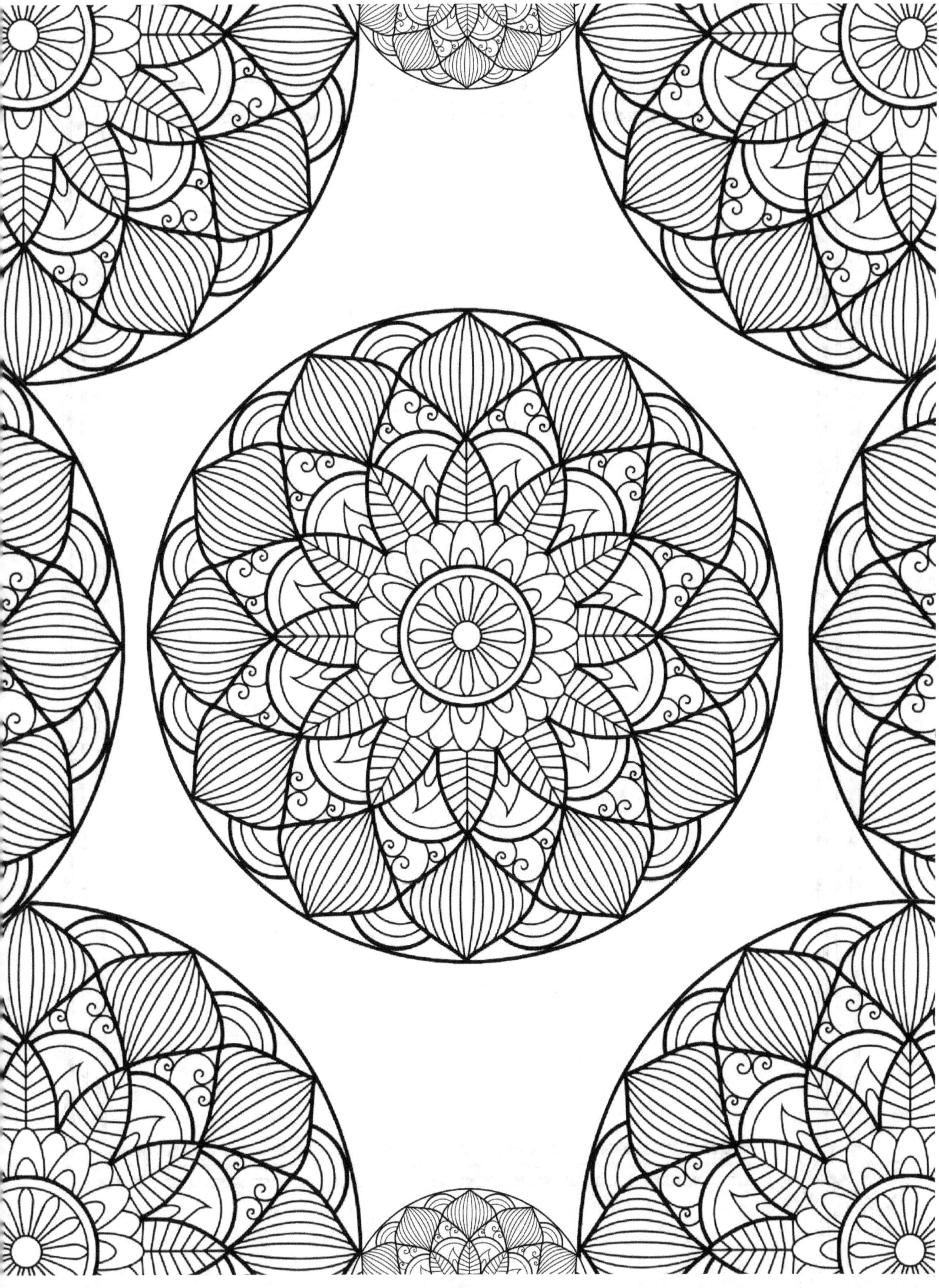

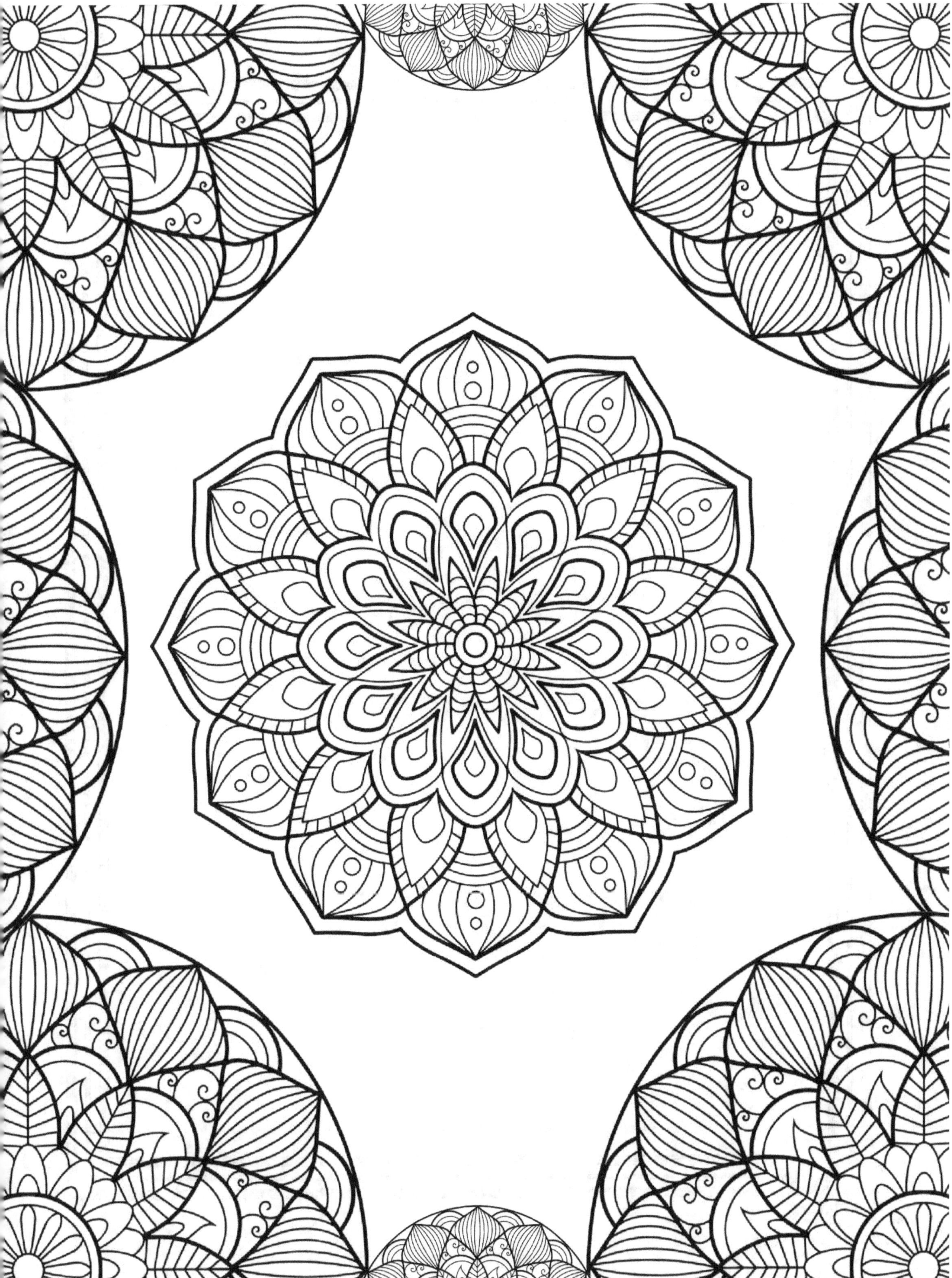

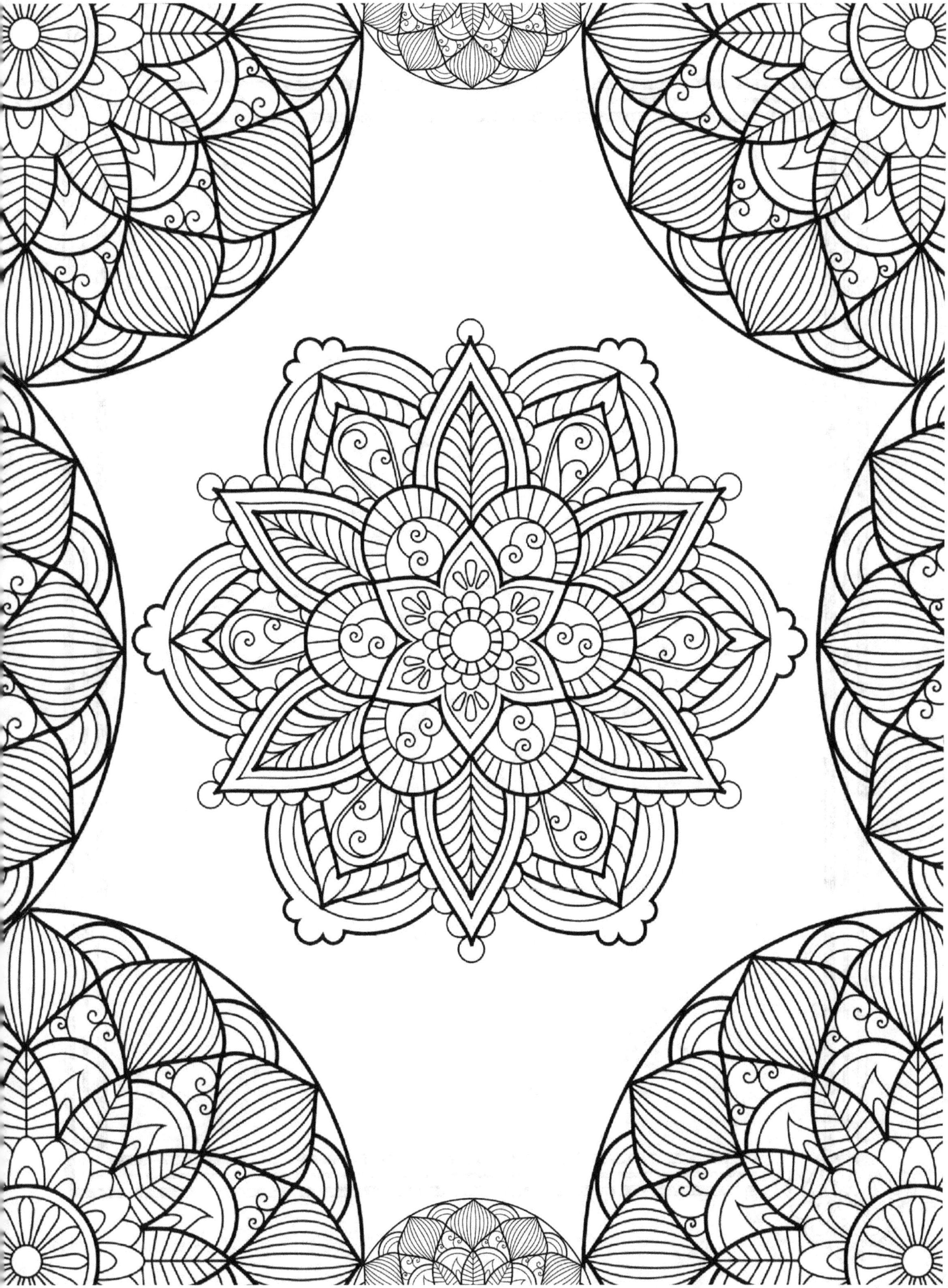

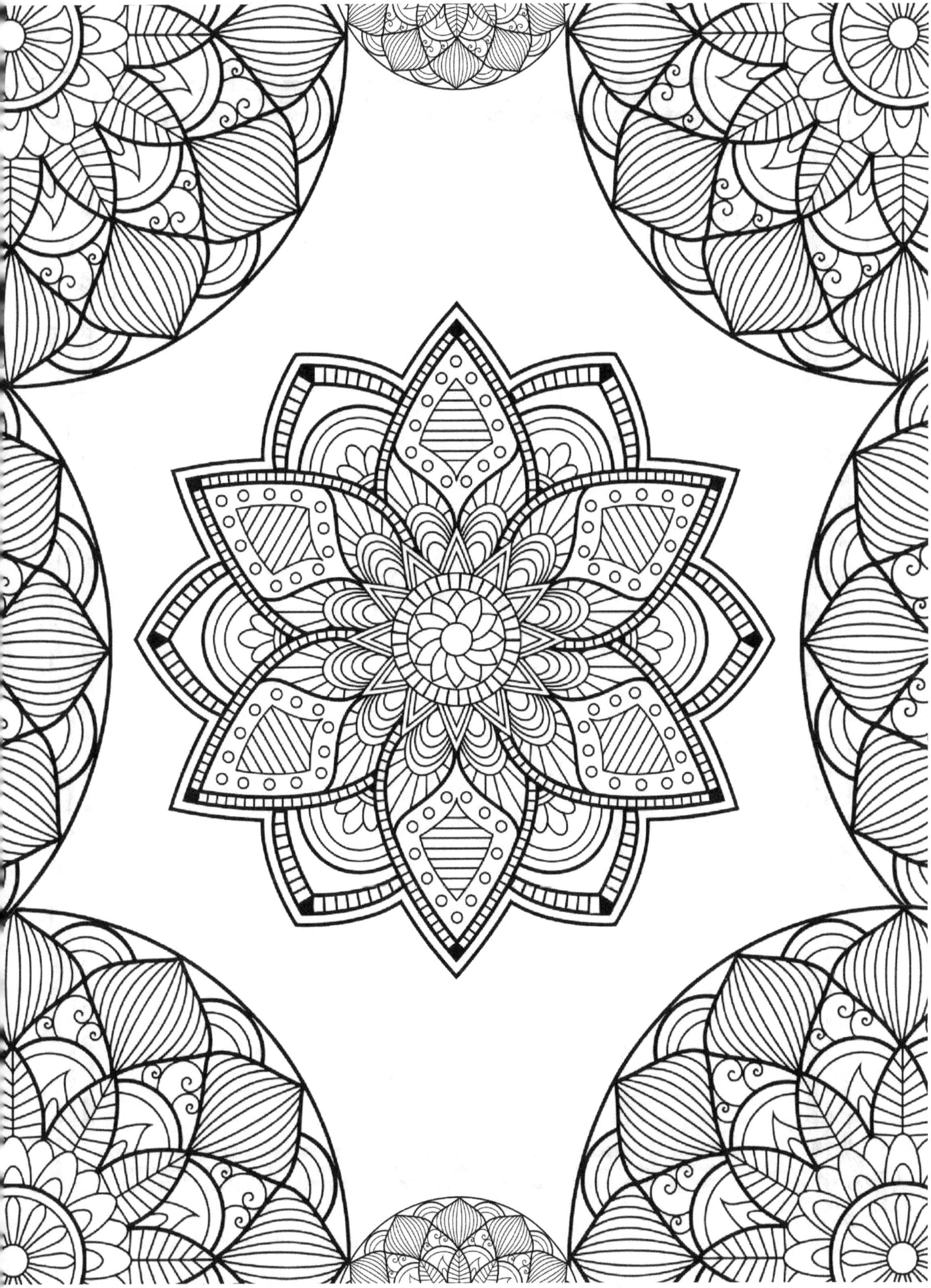

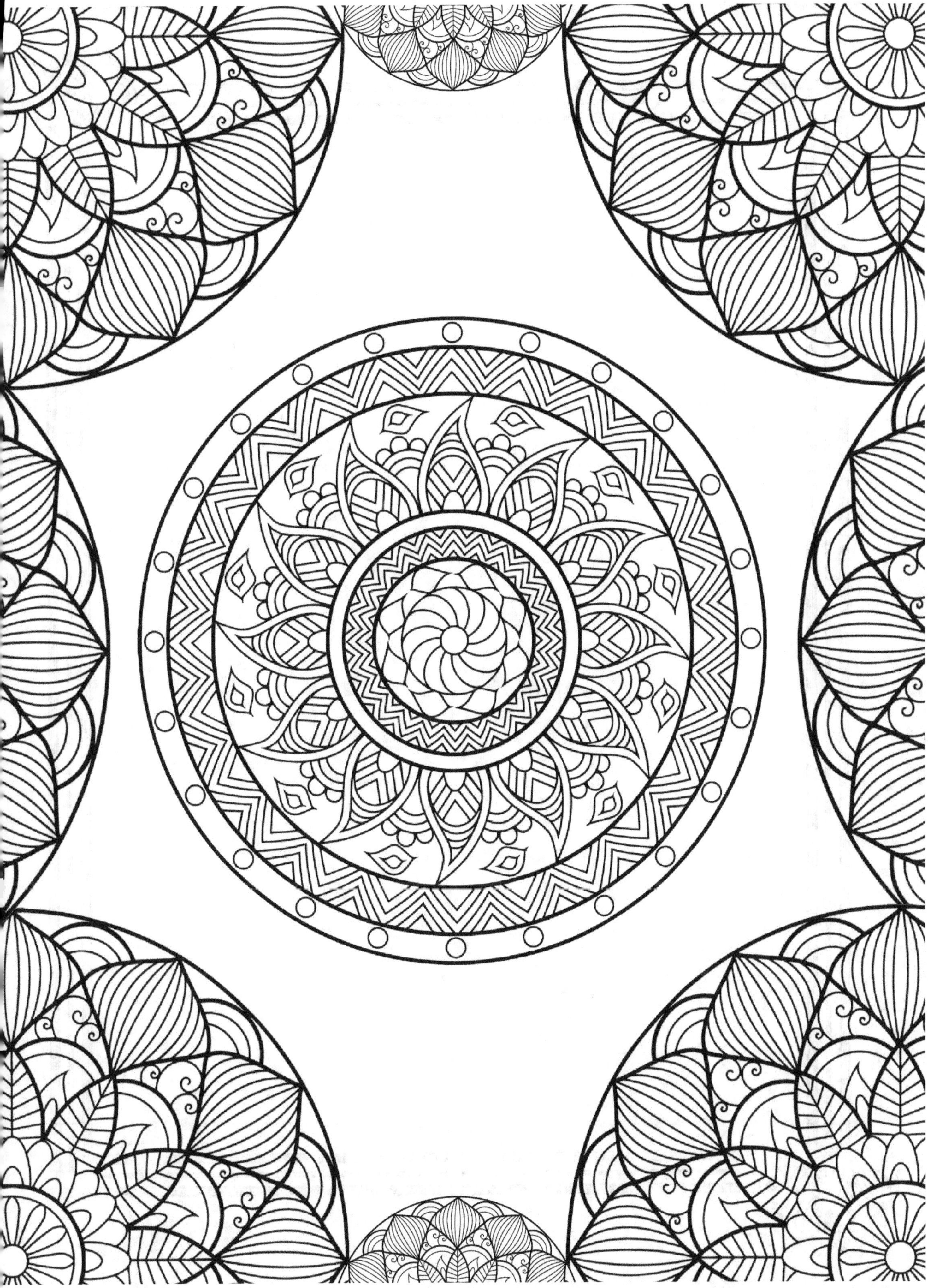

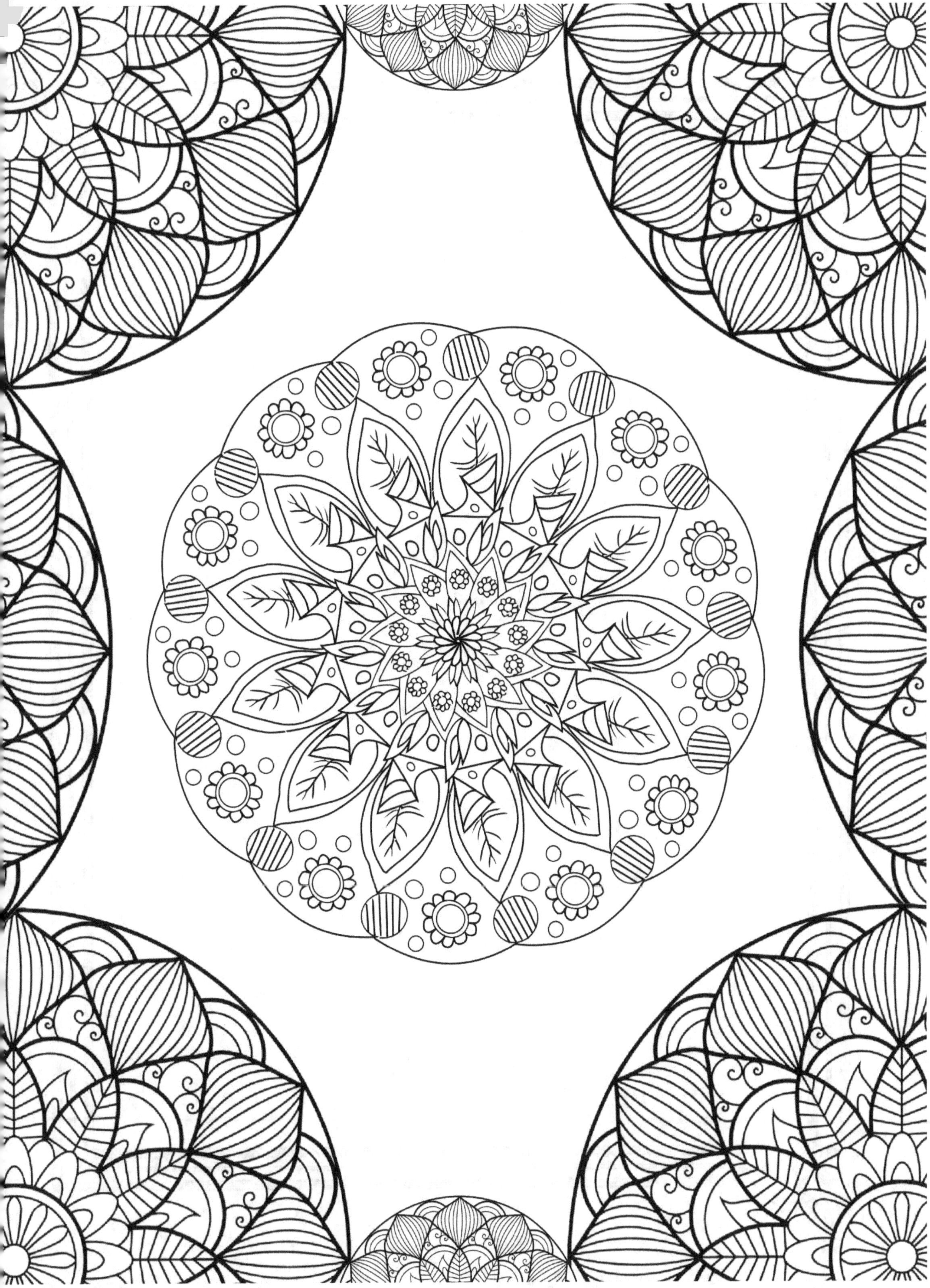

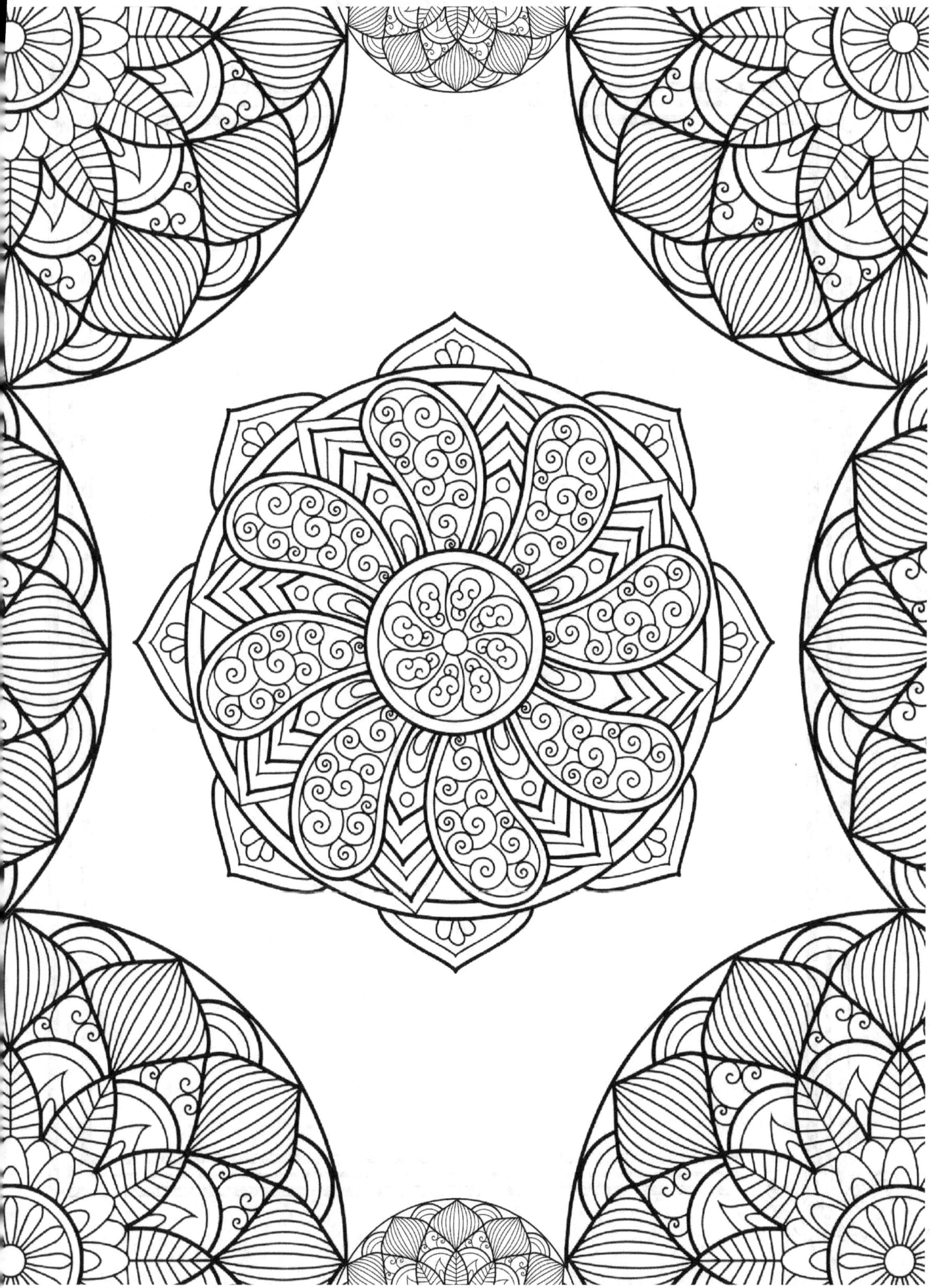

www.ingramcontent.com/pod-product-compliance
Lightning Source LLC
Chambersburg PA
CBHW080504220526
45465CB00006B/2374
9798649689045